The **Colonial Australian Culture Series** is a library of innovative, accessible, scholarly work that offers a compelling re-evaluation of Australia's all-too-proximate colonial past. Each title will focus on a particular cultural field, excavating often-forgotten historical sources to shed new light on aspects of our lives, practices and identities, tracing how these things transform over time. Future volumes will look at themes ranging from fashion, art and photography to cross-cultural encounters, Aboriginal resistance, and the colonial frontiers.

Ken Gelder is an Emeritus Professor of English at the University of Melbourne. His books include *Uncanny Australia: Sacredness and Identity in a Postcolonial Nation* (1998, with Jane M Jacobs), *Popular Fiction: The Logics and Practices of a Literary Field* (2004), *Subcultures: Cultural Histories and Social Practice* (2007), *After the Celebration: Australian Fiction 1989–2007* (2009, with Paul Salzman) and, with Rachael Weaver, *Colonial Australian Fiction* (2017) and *The Colonial Kangaroo Hunt* (2020).

Rachael Weaver is an ARC Future Fellow in English at the University of Tasmania and a 2024 Visiting Scholar at the State Library of New South Wales. She is the author of *The Criminal of the Century* (2006) and, with Ken Gelder, *The Colonial Journals, and the emergence of Australian literary culture* (2014), *Colonial Australian Fiction: Character Types, Social Formations and the Colonial Economy* (2017), and *The Colonial Kangaroo Hunt* (2020).

Colonial Adventure

KEN GELDER & RACHAEL WEAVER

Melbourne University Publishing acknowledges the traditional owners of the unceded land on which we work, learn and live: the Wurundjeri Woi-wurrung peoples of the Kulin nation. We pay respect to elders past, present and future, and acknowledge the importance of Indigenous knowledge.

MELBOURNE UNIVERSITY PRESS
An imprint of Melbourne University Publishing Limited
Level 1, 715 Swanston Street, Carlton, Victoria 3053, Australia
mup-contact@unimelb.edu.au
www.mup.com.au

First published 2024

Cover design by Pfisterer + Freeman
Text design and typesetting by Adala Studio
Cover image: S. Calvert (engraver) and Gibbs, Shallard and Co. (printer) after Oswald Rose Campbell, *Buckley Discovering Himself to the Early Settlers* (1869), colour wood engraving on paper, National Portrait Gallery of Australia
Printed in Australia by McPherson's Printing Group

A catalogue record for this book is available from the National Library of Australia

9780522879544 (paperback)
9780522879551 (ebook)

Contents

Acknowledgements

The Australian Research Council has long supported our collaborative work on things to do with colonial Australia and we're extremely appreciative. We're also grateful for support provided to this book by the School of Culture and Communication in the Faculty of Arts at the University of Melbourne. The *Colonial Australian Culture* board—Penelope Edmonds, Jane Lydon, Amanda Nettelbeck and Rachel Standfield—have been so good to work with, and we hope we can bring more publications into this series soon. Thanks, too, to the two readers who provided such generous and helpful feedback on the manuscript of this book.

We are thankful to everyone at Melbourne University Publishing for their dedication to this book, especially Nathan Hollier, who commissioned it; and Deborah Jordan, Foong Ling Kong and Duncan Fardon, who have reconfirmed MUP's commitment to the series itself. We're especially grateful to MUP senior editor Louise Stirling, our editor Sarina Rowell, and cover designer Pfisterer + Freeman for their care and skill in bringing this book to fruition.

Many thanks to Renée Joyce from the National Portrait Gallery of Australia for kindly arranging permission to reproduce part of *Buckley Discovering Himself to the Early Settlers* (1869).

Finally, love and thanks go to Hannah and Peter for being part of the journey (the 'adventure') as we put this book together and brought it to completion.

Note on Place Names

We have tried to honour Aboriginal place names wherever possible, following current practice to use dual names for Australian towns and cities, rivers and so on. We also try to identify Country where we can, which can sometimes be a bit of a challenge with novels and other works in the colonial archive that don't always prioritise accuracy. The AIATSIS Map of Indigenous Australia has been especially helpful in identifying nations and Country. Other sources—for example, the Tasmanian Aboriginal Centre's list of local place names and the Tasmanian Government's Aboriginal and Dual Names document—have also been very useful. There will inevitably be some errors here, for which we apologise.

We would like to acknowledge that we live and work on unceded Wurundjeri Woi Wurrung Country, and we convey our appreciation and respect to Elders of the Kulin nation, past and present.

Introduction

Colonial adventure is one of the grand narratives of colonisation. It gives colonisation its energy and purpose, its history and prehistory (since it can imagine colonisation before it actually happens), its achievements, and also its failures and disasters. This book is a literary, historical and cultural examination of colonial adventure that aims to offer a complex and nuanced appreciation of its function and definition. It looks at journals of exploration, travel memoirs, commentary and reportage, as well as adventure novels of one kind or another, and other forms of literary writing. Colonial adventure was expansive. Coming out of Europe in the early modern period—where we find the great imperial powers, Spain, Portugal, the Netherlands, Britain, etc—it took its protagonists into worlds far beyond the metropolitan centres, well beyond the realms of what was known and understood. One of those destinations was *Terra Australis Incognita* (Unknown Southern Land), which is the focus of this book. New encounters were important to colonial adventure, which often—but not always—aimed to illuminate the realities of outlying regions, taking readers to places they were unlikely ever to visit themselves. Many colonial adventure narratives—the accounts found in ship's journals, for example—placed great value on the transmission of authentic knowledges about Indigenous people, native flora and fauna, landscapes, weather patterns and so on. But colonisation always came in their wake.

Colonial adventure emphasised the capacity of Europeans to move freely, although not unproblematically, through the remoter parts of the world, landing on distant shores with—in many cases—a remarkable confidence, an unshakeable sense of their own racial superiority, and a hope, or assumption, that what they saw would one day belong to them. In 1911 the German sociologist Georg Simmel wrote about the adventurer as a 'social type', casting adventure as an existential form of re-enchantment with the world that is at the same time (and literally) a departure from what he called 'the usual continuity of ... life'.[1] This account assumes that the adventurer, 'after a long and unfamiliar detour', would finally return home and life would continue much as it was.[2] But if we think about *colonial* adventure, another of Simmel's 'social types' may be more useful here. 'The Stranger' (1908) introduces a figure who precisely embodies the expansive ambitions of colonisation—namely, the trader or speculator. As Simmel puts it, unlike 'the wanderer who comes today and goes tomorrow', the stranger is someone 'who comes today and *stays* tomorrow'.[3] We can say something similar about the agents of colonisation: that although they may experience many adventures (and long and unfamiliar detours) along the way, when they arrive at their destination they generally do not leave.

Even so, colonial adventure doesn't always go in a straight line—it can indeed make space for wandering, for meandering, or for losing one's way altogether. Colonial adventure is a matter of speculation, of weighing up whether the risks involved in a hazardous journey are going to pay off (in terms of wealth acquisition, trade routes, resources, land, wellbeing, etc). The speculator/adventurer is therefore important to this book, as we'll see in Chapter 1 and Chapter 5. Colonial adventure was not just to do with visiting distant places; it also involved opening up new sites for investment and, in order to succeed, sanctioning the often-unlimited exploitation of people and resources. It rides on the back of what Cedric J Robinson called 'racial capitalism', which has its modern origins in the early sixteenth century, when the Portuguese first transported West African slaves across the Atlantic.[4] The subsequent genocide of Indigenous people in the Americas, the consolidation of the slave trade as a viable commercial enterprise, and the establishment of immensely profitable plantations for slaves to work on—sugar, in particular—were all 'central to the development of eighteenth-century Atlantic capitalism'.[5] By the nineteenth century, as Kris Manjapra writes, 'the colonial forces of racial capitalism [had] transformed the majority of human beings on earth into slaves, coolies, bonded labourers, or low-paid wage workers'.[6] The Australian colonies played their role in all this. We need only think of the dispossession and long-term systemic exploitation of Aboriginal workers in the cattle and sheep industries—or in the pearling industry, which in 1881 the Western Australian governor, William Robinson, regarded as 'a state of things little short of slavery'.[7] Across the colonies, Aboriginal people, children especially, were taken from their families and communities, forced into institutional and domestic servitude, and subjected to physical and sexual abuse by white administrators and property owners who might, at the same time, represent themselves as their 'appointed saviours' and protectors.[8]

We can also think about the transportation of convicts, which between 1788 and 1868 saw over 163 000 people shipped out to the colonies as an unpaid, incarcerated labour force, conscripted into work for 'immigrant capitalists' in a disciplinary system that itself often seemed 'more like slavery'.[9] In Chapter 2, we talk about convict transportation and convict adventures, noting a number of connections to the slave trade and sugar plantations in the Caribbean. But other coerced workers were conscripted to the colonies as well. The first Pacific islanders were shipped to the southern coast of New South Wales in April 1847, to work on stations owned by the wealthy colonial merchant and pastoralist Benjamin Boyd. Boyd's father, Edward, had been directly involved in the transatlantic slave trade and fought against its abolition.[10] When sugar and cotton plantations were established in Queensland in the early1860s, the often-violent recruitment of Pacific islanders to the colony—known as 'blackbirding'—quickly escalated. Tracey Banivanua-Mar has noted that from 1863, 'around sixty thousand men, women, and children from diverse islands in the southwestern Pacific laboured for bonded periods of at least three years in the burgeoning sugar industry of ... Queensland', providing 'cost-neutral, coercible, and coloured labour' that was seen to be essential to the future of a plantation economy.[11]

In August 1863 the pastoralist and merchant trader Robert Towns (Townsville is named after him) 'recruited' seventy-three Pacific islanders to work on his cotton plantation along the Logan River, south of Meeanjin/Brisbane. His superintendent was Henry Ross Lewin, a notorious blackbirder. Lewin was under investigation by the Royal Navy's George Palmer, commander of the HMS *Rosario*. Palmer's fascinating record of his experiences, *Kidnapping in the South Seas* (1871), reported the discovery of a large number of men from the Banks Islands, north of Vanuatu, on board a schooner, the *Daphne*, anchored at Levuka, the colonial capital of Fiji. Although it was under licence, the boat, Palmer writes, was 'fitted up precisely like an African slaver, minus the irons, with 100 natives on board .... they were stark naked, and had not even a mat to lie upon ...'[12] He brought his case against Lewin—'who I heard of at every island I visited, as a notorious man stealer'[13]—to the Admiralty Court of New South Wales, which exonerated the Queensland government 'from any connivance at the practice of slave-stealing or slavery in any shape'.[14] Lewin himself was shot dead by islanders on his own plantation in Tanna, Vanuatu, in April 1874.

In the late 1890s the Australian trader and adventure writer Louis Becke published a number of stories about the 'recruitment'—a loaded term disguising acts of coercion, violent kidnappings, killings, etc—of islander labourers in the Pacific, usually set back in the 1870s, when Lewin and others were active there. Around the time Lewin was killed, Becke (still a teenager) sailed with the American blackbirder and swindler William 'Bully' Hayes, on the *Leonora*. The ship was wrecked in a storm off the island of Kosrae in Micronesia, with Hayes and Becke remaining there for several months; 'Hayes made himself ruler of the island', Becke remarked in an autobiographical note, 'and he and I had a little quarrel'.[15] Hayes became an important figure in Becke's adventure fiction, a 'buccaneer' he both admired and was appalled by. In 'The Wreck of the Leonora', from *Ridan the Devil and Other Stories* (1899), he wrote: 'Had he lived in the times of ... [William] Dampier, he [Hayes] would have been a hero, for he was a man born to command and lead'.[16] (We'll look at Dampier himself—as well as some shipwrecks—in Chapter 1.)

Becke's stories about the recruitment of Pacific labourers for plantations in both the Pacific and the Australian colonies were much less admiring, although they ran the risk of relishing the violence and brutality they described, or exposed. In 'Collier: The "Blackbirder"', from *Pacific Tales* (1896), the recruitment boats are 'splashed with blood from stem to stem' as islanders put up a spirited resistance (a version of a Caribbean slave revolt) and the recruiters take a gruesome revenge. 'I swore to God', the narrator says, 'that once I got out of that barque I would never ship in such a bloody trade again'.[17] The *Pacific Island Labourers Act* of 1901 saw the outlawing of the use of Pacific labourers, and the forced deportation of many of those islanders who had been working and living for so long on the colonies' plantations: one expression of the newly federated nation's White Australia policy. Becke carried on writing about 'blackbirding' regardless, in stories such as 'On the "Joys" of Recruiting "Blackbirds"', from *The Call of the South* (1908), and 'A "Blackbirding" Incident', from *The Pearl Divers of Roncador Reef* (1908). By now, the recruitment of Pacific islanders is a distant historical moment, with Becke's fiction looking back (nostalgically?) at the excitement and violent excesses of what is cast as a pre-Federation anomaly. For Becke, the colonial adventure was 'blackbirding' itself.

~

Colonial adventure mostly had specific destinations in mind and worked towards specific outcomes: status, profit, land, labour, colonisation. In Chapter 5, we look at the journals of two explorers—Thomas Mitchell and George Grey—who set out across Country with the aim of charting and securing land. The hope of discovering an inland sea is a central theme in this chapter, which ends by looking at two colonial 'speculative' novels that imagine a huge body of water in the Australian interior—where protagonists also ruthlessly pursue unlimited wealth. As we have noted, however, colonial adventure was not always so unremittingly driven towards a particular goal. Adventurers could wander off or get lost along the way. They might get shipwrecked (as Becke was) and become castaways, occasionally for lengthy periods of time: another version of Simmel's 'long and unfamiliar detour'. Events like these—unexpected, accidental, difficult to predict—are fundamental to the dynamics of the colonial adventure. Chapter 1 looks at early navigators who lost their way, and explorers such as William Dampier who were lost and cast away several times over. Earlier speculative novels from the seventeenth and eighteenth centuries (such as Jonathan Swift's *Gulliver's Travels*) imagined visiting Australia by mistake or misfortune. This book will also show that colonial adventurers would sometimes go off course by choice. Chapter 2 will look at convict adventures, where convicts determined to leave the colonies and get as far away as they possibly could. The first great convict escape, in March 1791, involved the theft of a six-oar boat, with the convict crew (and two children) rowing all the way from Warrane/ Sydney Cove to West Timor. In Chapter 3, we look at transported convicts, such as William Buckley and John Graham, who escaped penal servitude to live with Aboriginal people; in some cases, for many years. Chapter 4 looks at bushrangers—John Caesar, Michael Howe, Mary Cockerill, and many others—who left colonial settlements to pose an active threat to local governance and order. These escapes and insurrections resonate with Cedric Robinson's comments about the first wave of new world revolts in the Caribbean, where slaves fleeing the plantations, rather than 'overthrow[ing] capitalism', 'created maroon settlements, ran away, became outliers, and tried to find a way home, even if it meant death'.[18] In the Australian colonies, absconding convicts, bushrangers and castaways certainly didn't overthrow colonisation (since it couldn't be stopped); but they did offer outlying moments of refusal or dissent, as well the possibility of other ways of living and understanding. Colonial adventure was not always overtly in the service of empire, and didn't always champion the dispossession of Aboriginal people and the forced acquisition of their land. Adventure narratives might be thought of as unreflective, a formulaic chronicle of characters moving quickly from one obstacle to the next. But, as we've noted, they could also transmit information about people and places never before seen; some of that information might even disturb the ideologies that colonisation relied on. These are reasons why colonial adventure—for all its racism and rawness of perspective —is still worth looking at today.

CHAPTER 1

Ocean Voyages, Real and Imaginary

THE OCEAN VOYAGE provided colonial adventure with many of its key tropes: the initial act of leaving home and homeland; risk and speculation; obstacles, discovery, encounter; and possibly some level of self-transformation along the way. It could indeed be illuminating for some, although devastating for many others; it was confident in its purpose, but it is worth noting that it did not always know precisely where it was heading or where it might end up. Early voyages to the so-called East Indies (archipelagic South-East Asia) saw the often-violent establishment of colonial outposts and trade routes, with various empire-building European nations competing with each other for spices and other valuables. Founded in 1602, the Dutch East India Company (VOC) was the first company in the world to make equity shares publicly available (on the Amsterdam Stock Exchange).[1] It soon came to monopolise trade in the region, making immense profits. But its agents' first encounters with *Terra Australis Incognita* were either accidental or a misunderstanding of where they were and what they were actually looking at. On one of its more exploratory voyages in the region, the crew of Willem Janszoon's VOC ship *Duyfken* produced a chart of the west coast of Cape York (from Anggamudi Country down to Anguthimri Country), thinking it was the west coast of New Guinea. This is generally regarded as the first map to show any part of the Australian continent. In 1616 Dirk Hartog's VOC ship *Eendracht* was blown off course in the Indian Ocean on the way to Batavia (now Jakarta); he spent a couple of days stranded at what is now called Gutharraguda/Shark Bay in Western Australia before sailing on to the more familiar eastern Indonesian port of Makassar.

Navigational technologies and techniques were still evolving at this time, and ships were vulnerable to the effects of severe weather, as well as to mutinous crews, sickness and so on. Abel Janszoon Tasman was a VOC commander and merchant who lived in Batavia. In 1642 his ships *Heemskerck* and *Zeehaen* set sail for Mauritius in the Indian Ocean. On the return journey, heavy winds made them alter their course; they sailed well south of the Australian continent and eventually sighted what is now known as lutruwita/Tasmania. Tasman planted a Dutch flag and named the island Van Diemen's Land (*Anthoonij van Diemenslandt*), after the governor-general of Batavia, who had authorised the exploration. (The name was officially changed to Tasmania, after Tasman, on 1 January 1856.) Many years later, in 1895, the Hobart-born archivist and historian James Backhouse Walker read to the Royal Society of Tasmania what he claimed was the first English account of Tasman's life and voyages. For Backhouse, Tasman's 'discovery' of lutruwita/Tasmania

> was no chance adventure. It was the result of a steady policy. It was the outcome of the adventurous energy which in the 16th and 17th centuries created the Dutch Republic; gave to Holland her Colonial Empire; and—not content with her possession of the Eastern Archipelago—sent out her sailors to search for a new world in the unknown regions of the mysterious South.[2]

This is a late colonial view of colonisation as an activity sanctioned by the state as well as by a rich and powerful company, a purposeful, systematic and predictable process (like an already established trade route): 'no chance adventure'. On the other hand, colonisation itself is driven by an 'adventurous energy' that can certainly be blown off course as it heads into 'unknown' and 'mysterious' places—and, in many cases, struggles to get back home again. The tension between these two positions will be important to this book's understanding of what colonial adventure is, and what it does.

Can we think about James Cook as an adventurer? From a European perspective, he was perhaps the greatest adventurer of all, embarking on what Nicholas Thomas calls three 'extraordinary voyages' around the world—the first of which marked the very beginnings of Australia's colonisation by the British.[3] One of the two ships in his second voyage was in fact named HMS *Adventure*, under the command of the British navigator Tobias Furneaux. When the *Adventure* became separated from Cook's *Resolution* during bad weather in March 1773, Furneaux misread almost every location around the south coast of Tasmania, but named the site at which his ship anchored Adventure Bay, on the east side of lunawanna-allonah/Bruny Island. The British novelist William Howitt, who travelled to the Victorian goldfields in the early 1850s, later characterised these navigational errors as 'Furneaux's adventures in Van Diemen's Land' in his book *The History of Discovery in Australia, Tasmania, and New Zealand* (1865).[4]

Cook's three voyages were all commissioned by the state—the British Admiralty and George III—giving them an official status that placed them squarely in the framework of colonial exploration and the ongoing expansion of the British empire. He was given (secret) instructions by the Admiralty, outlining the routes he needed to follow and explore. Each voyage was meant to produce precise charts and accurate scientific descriptions of, in many cases, previously unknown places, populations, species and so on. But things did sometimes go wrong along the way. The *Endeavour* ran aground on the Great Barrier Reef in June 1770, and Cook was forced to jettison a significant amount of ballast, including six cannons (retrieved in 1969 by a research team, and now held in museums in New Zealand, Australia, the United States and England). The third voyage, of course, would bring about Cook's death at Kealakekua Bay, on the west coast of the island of Hawai'i. The *Resolution* was supposed to have left the island, but a storm forced it to return for repairs. Relations with the islanders quickly soured. A longboat went missing and Cook retaliated by attempting to abduct a ruling chief, Kalaniʻōpuʻu. Even a state-sanctioned, well-planned voyage commanded by an honoured representative of the crown could become hazardous, with outcomes that were not always possible to predict. This is in fact one way of understanding adventure, as a journey and set of experiences filled with mishaps and obstacles, beset by things that go wrong, not least because locations, encounters and situations could indeed be continually (and often wilfully) misread or misunderstood. In this sense, adventure can also have a lot to do with misadventure.

The journals recording a ship's voyage—especially if it was far-reaching—became vibrant source texts that framed exploration as an adventure narrative built around travel, discovery and encounter. They might be written by the captain—Cook kept meticulous journals—or by members of the scientific community who would join the voyage and register their own discoveries along the way. The naturalist Sir Joseph Banks kept a journal on Cook's first voyage; so did the talented species artist Sydney Parkinson. Bernard Smith has commented on the importance of ship's journals as an 'empirical' daily register of scientific observations, sightings, events, encounters and so on. They can be fascinating and a bit mundane at the same time. Like the route a ship was supposed to take, journals were a requirement of the state, an official and supposedly reliable record of everything that happened during the voyage: 'By 1588', Smith writes, 'British explorers were already being advised in their official instructions to keep daily diaries ... From its foundation in 1660 the Royal Society appreciated the value of journals kept by seaman and travellers ...'[5]

Credibility was therefore important. A few years before John Hawkesworth's best-selling 1773 publication of Cook's journal of his first voyage, Captain John Byron published *A Voyage Round the World, In His Majesty's Ship The Dolphin* (1766). Byron—the grandfather of Lord Byron, the poet—was commissioned by the Royal Navy to establish a British military base in the South Atlantic (this would later be the Falkland Islands). Twenty-five years earlier, in 1741, Byron had sailed to South America in the *Wager*, one of a large squadron of British warships. Separated from the others and with an already mutinous crew, the *Wager* was shipwrecked during a severe storm on what became known as Wager Island, off the south-western coast of Chile. This was the beginning of Byron's adventure (or, rather, a 'series of unfortunate adventures'); his narrative of the five years he spent trying to survive in the region and get home again was published in 1768, to popular acclaim.[6] But his later journal, *A Voyage Round the World*, is different: a more prosaic, matter-of-fact, diary-like chronicle of what was at the time the fastest circumnavigation of the world (in less than two years). 'The Reader in this Work has a Right to expect Truth, and will not be disappointed', Byron wrote, clearly valuing credibility above everything else.[7] But this particular ship's journal also contained an account of a 'gigantic race of Patagonians', a myth that had circulated since the Portuguese explorer Magellan's arrival in the region in 1520. The fabulous tale was true, Byron seemed to suggest: 'the discovery of the gigantic race of Patagonians is one of the most curious and extraordinary particulars of this voyage'.[8]

Given the tasks assigned both to him and the scientific community on board, Cook needed to invest his own voyage journals with an authority—and truth—that properly reflected their sense of obligation to their country. The credibility of what he wrote down day by day is one reason why so many objects and specimens at various destinations were collected, classified, described in methodical detail and brought back home for further analysis. At seventeen, the German-born George Forster accompanied his naturalist father on Cook's second voyage around the world from 1772 to 1775: a voyage charged by the British Admiralty with establishing whether a great south land actually existed. The question of who should write an official account of the voyage became complicated; in the event, George, the son, went ahead and published his own *A Voyage Round the World*, based on his father's journals, in 1777. Unhappy at the way Hawkesworth had (mis)treated his account of his first voyage, Cook had himself been keeping a careful record of the second, later edited by John Douglas. But which account of the voyage had the most authority, Cook's or Forster's? Nicholas Thomas and Oliver Berghof regard Forster's version as 'unconstrained' by the Admiralty's instructions, and therefore more at liberty to meander into philosophical and other kinds of discussions (although not necessarily to make things up). On the other hand, the care Cook exercised over his own journal 'suggests ... that he was mindful of the importance of narrating the voyage in a credible fashion'.[9] Thomas and Berghof go on to note the importance, to Cook, of authoring a cartographically accurate, scientifically reliable narrative, one that didn't deviate from the realities of the voyage itself. 'Given the extent to which voyagers had made mistakes, circulated fancies like the Patagonian giants [as John Byron did, above], and advanced fraudulent claims', they write, 'the empirical creditworthiness of a voyage publication was not [just] a nicety of proper reportage, but a project of careful and persuasive writing, and it was hardly less fundamental to the success of a voyage than the navigational accomplishment itself'.[10] A ship's journal that takes liberties with the actualities of a voyage is a bit like a ship that gets blown off course.

Were the journals Cook's 'extraordinary voyages' produced adventure narratives? In an obvious sense, they certainly were, since adventure narratives from Homer's *Odyssey* onwards have tracked the experiences of their protagonists as they travel far away from home to places unknown and/or make their laborious, obstacle-ridden way back again. But the official status of Cook's voyages, as journeys of exploration in the service of the state and under the state's instructions, places certain limits on their adventurous capacity. It is possible, instead, to think of adventure itself more as a matter of detour or deviation—from one's home, from an authorised route, from official instructions; or from credibility itself, from an authorised truth. A key figure worth discussing along these lines is a much earlier explorer who also circumnavigated the world three times, William Dampier.

Dampier's first circumnavigation began in 1679, on ships commanded by buccaneers (who were not sanctioned by the state) and privateers (who had permission from the state to raid enemy ships; mostly Spanish ones, in this case). There are tensions or disputes here between state authorisation and commercial and entrepreneurial self-interest. Early in 1686 Dampier joined the crew of the so-called 'reluctant buccaneer' Charles Swan's ship, *Cygnet*, embarking on a turbulent, mutinous voyage. When the crew seized Swan's journal and read his opinion of them—an accurate record of his feelings? —they put him ashore on Mindanao in the Philippines and Captain Read took command. Dampier was already thinking about the 'vast tract of *Terra Australis* which bounds the *South Sea*' and is 'yet undiscovered'.[11] Not long afterwards, the *Cygnet* was blown off course by strong winds, landing on the north-west coast of Australia (New Holland at the time) in January 1688.

On land, Dampier recorded his notorious impressions of the local Jaburrara (or Yapurarra) people: 'The Inhabitants of this Country are the miserablest People in the World', he wrote, a starkly racist judgement that has since been reproduced many times over by the various explorers, visitors, settlers and commentators who came in his wake. Dampier thought these 'New Hollanders' lived in a pure state of nature, without possessions or property—a view that would later find expression in the French philosopher Jean-Jacques Rousseau's reflections on 'natural man' in *Discourse on Inequality* (1754) and go on to influence the colonial legal doctrine of *terra nullius*. For Dampier, Jaburrara people seemed to have 'no Houses, but lye in the open Air, without any covering; the Earth being their Bed, and the Heaven their Canopy'.[12] He attempted to give a brief description of some Jaburrara customs and behavioural traits; as Shino Konishi has noted, he was in fact the first visitor 'to describe the Aboriginal face in any detail' for British readers.[13] But he also seemed to realise that much of what he (briefly) saw was completely beyond him: for example, 'How they get their fire, I know not'.[14] The Jaburrara were not hostile and there was no conflict with the crew. But Dampier's encounter, the first recorded British encounter with Aboriginal people, was profoundly unenlightening for him: 'we could not understand one word that they said'.[15] Of all the places Dampier visited, Australia/New Holland was the least familiar, the most opaque. It frustrated his ethnographic/scientific aspirations to understand and record the customs and manners of the people he saw.

As the *Cygnet* headed west, Dampier found himself in intense disagreement with Captain Read and resolved to leave the ship. Put ashore with several crew members on one of the Nicobar Islands, north-west of Singapore, he was effectively marooned. The experience of being marooned provides another key trope in colonial adventure narratives, as we will see. In voyage narratives, it produces a kind of hiatus in the journey, a pause or deviation that generates its own forms of adventurous activity. The word *maroon* probably comes from the Spanish *cimarrón*, which originally referred 'to cattle that escaped colonial farms on Hispaniola' and became wild.[16] Soon afterwards, it began to be applied to runaway slaves. It appeared in English in 1666—just a couple of decades before Dampier was put ashore and left to fend for himself—in John Davies' translation of Charles de Rochefort's *The History of the Caribby-Islands*, which noted that if slaves 'be treated with excessive severity, they will run away, and get into the Mountains and Forests, where they live like so many Beasts; then they are call'd *Marons*, that is to say, Savages ...'.[17] Dampier, of course, was not a runaway slave. But he was certainly an absconder who wanted to free himself from another's command. He also aimed to trade ambergris on the island, hoping to gain 'a considerable Fortune to my self'.[18]

After around five weeks on the island, Dampier and the crew members got hold of a canoe and prepared to row around 300 kilometres south to the East India Company depot Achin (now Aceh), on the northern tip of Sumatra. The boat overturned at their first attempt, and they were soaked. 'I had nothing of value but my Journal and some Drafts of Land, of my own taking, which I much prized, and which I had hitherto carefully preserved'.[19] Like Cook, Dampier had made copious notes about the places he visited and the things he saw on his voyages; this was his own ship's journal, a chronicle of everything he had been through. An amateur naturalist, he also took pains to describe fruits and plants and species in great detail, alongside his account of the various human dramas and conflicts on and off the *Cygnet*. The canoe journey was hazardous and challenging but expertly navigated. At Achin, Dampier recovered his health and spent two more years away from home, mostly working as a gunner for the East India Company. 'I began to long after my native Country,' he wrote, 'after so tedious a Ramble from it'.[20] The word *ramble* suggests something unplanned and meandering, quite different from a route that dutifully and purposefully follows the instructions of the Admiralty. It also suggests a writing style that moves (not always predictably) from one place to another, which is what so many adventure narratives—and ship's journals—tend to do. It suggests aimlessness as well, as if Dampier, for all his remarkable navigational skills, didn't always know where he was going or what his destination would finally be.

This is not quite the determined journey of colonisation, and Dampier certainly didn't claim land for the British empire in the way that Cook later did. But he did follow established colonial trade routes, and aimed to acquire land and extract precious commodities. In this sense, Dampier *did* know where he was going and how to get there. Before he returned to England in September 1691, he purchased a slave from Mindanao in the Philippines, a 'Painted Prince'—a heavily tattooed man—named Jeoly. Dampier wanted to profit from Jeoly by getting him to help set up a new trade route to islands south of the Philippines, rich in spices, gold and other valuables. He eventually took Jeoly back with him to England and, having lost almost everything at the end of his long voyage, sold him on to (or, in some accounts, was conned by) a business that exhibited the decorated slave, now called Prince Giolo, as a public curiosity. Geraldine Barnes has noted that Dampier himself combined a sense of curiosity (about the rest of the world) with a buccaneer's driven ambition to 'gett wealth', as he put it.[21] But in England, Jeoly was reduced to little more than a human embodiment of Dampier's mercantile colonial ambitions. Six years later, and with the backing of the Royal Society, Dampier published his ship's journal in London, as *A New Voyage Round the World* (1697). The manuscript was significantly rewritten and modified during this time; it went on to become a bestseller (with two more editions that year) and 'established a new standard for exploratory travel writing, combining a keen eye for detail with a plain, unembellished prose style'.[22]

In his book *Dampier's Monkey* (2010), Adrian Mitchell places the privateer/explorer outside the frame of colonisation precisely because his voyages did indeed seem to ramble or meander. Dampier, Mitchell writes, was

> a sea-wayfarer sailing the seas of the world with no special destination, no quest other than the ongoingness of the voyage ... He did not attempt to own what he took up ... his vocabulary commemorates not so much his own

> experiences as an out-of-the-way life shared with other old piratical sea-dogs and freebooters. One curious corollary is that there is not much of the coloniser in this attitude. He was more given to the hit-and-run raids along the coast and up and down the sea-lanes.[23]

There is some truth in this view, but it romanticises Dampier, and sets him too far apart from the structures, routes and ambitions of colonial trade and mercantile expansion that had so much to do with where he went and what he did there. A voyage journal like Dampier's is certainly an example of what Barbara Fuchs calls 'itinerant texts': that is, narratives that move fluently from one place to another, and from one event to another. They have this in common with the picaresque genre, with its travelling (anti-)hero who is often also the narrator.[24] For Fuchs, the picaresque presents an 'unreliable voice' that can challenge 'the authority of the witness' through exaggeration, misunderstanding, self-promotion and so on.[25] The voyage journal, however, sometimes blurs the differences between these two things, making it hard to tell what has credibility and what doesn't.

We can see this in Dampier's account of his second visit to New Holland in 1699, a journey with a clear, authorised destination. Dampier asked for two ships and three years of supplies for the trip. But the Admiralty gave him just one small warship, the *Roebuck*, and '50 men and boys'.[26] In his Preface to the journal of the voyage, Dampier wrote that people seemed to assume it was easy to travel to unknown places far away, not realising that 'Seamen are apt ... in long Voyages [to] know not whither they are going' and constantly risk 'the Hazard of all outward Accidents in strange and unknown Seas'.[27] This is the adventurous aspect of an ocean voyage. But Dampier was defensive in his Preface as well, wanting to assert his authority as a credible witness to events. He complained about accusations that he had plagiarised from other voyage journals, 'as if I was not my self the Author of what I write ....'[28] He also noted the accusation that because he never really stayed long in one place, he couldn't properly account for what he saw: 'there are some who are apt to slight my Accounts and Descriptions of Things, as if it was an easie Matter and of little or no Difficulty to do all that I have done, to visit little more than the Coasts of unknown Countries, and make short and imperfect Observations of Things only near the Shore'.[29] These comments are close to Mitchell's, as if Dampier was indeed more like a passing visitor than a coloniser who intended to stay. But he also wanted his voyage narrative to have credibility and a lasting effect, taking an artist with him to illustrate the things he saw. The *Roebuck* was blown off course—now a generic feature of these early voyages—but Dampier finally arrived on the west coast of New Holland in early August 1699. He spent the next couple of months charting the coast from the place he named Shark's Bay to Lagrange Bay, south of Rubibi/Broome.

Dampier usually described with some degree of accuracy the birds and fish he saw. But in Western Australia, he reported a more peculiar sighting: 'The Land-Animals that we saw here were only a sort of Racoons ... a larger and uglier Head ... at the Rump, instead of a Tail there, they had a stump of a Tail, which appear'd like another Head ... this Creature seem'd by this means to have a Head at each end'.[30] It's difficult to tell what marsupials Dampier was looking at here; perhaps he saw female wombats with infants in their rear-facing pouch (except they don't resemble racoons), or perhaps this was simply a moment that veered into something more fabulous than true. Further north, he was attacked by local Aboriginal (probably Karajarri) people and discharged his gun to frighten them off. But they attacked again and Dampier shot a young man, wounding him. 'I return'd back with my Men', he wrote, 'designing to attempt the Natives no further, being very sorry for what happen'd already. They took up their wounded Companion ...'.[31] Dampier repeated his earlier harsh assessment of the people he called New Hollanders and—unable to find fresh water—left the Western Australian coast in September, setting sail for Timor. Ross Gibson wrote about Dampier in his early book *The Diminishing Paradise* (1984), where he noted that such explorers entertained 'optimistic fantasies' about *Terra Australis* while witnessing an often sobering or disillusioning reality.[32] But Dampier was himself in poor shape, and the *Roebuck* was worm-eaten, leaking and barely seaworthy. The ship foundered near the island of Ascension in the South Atlantic in February 1700; the crew were marooned on that island for around six weeks. When he finally got back to England, a naval court found Dampier guilty of cruelly mistreating (by caning) his lieutenant, George Fisher. He was fined three years' salary and dismissed from the British navy. Soon afterwards, he returned to privateering.

~

If adventure narratives are defined not just by their destination but by what happens when travellers go off course, when they get lost or become a castaway, then Dampier's journals certainly qualify. He was marooned himself a couple of times, although for relatively brief periods. He was also closely linked to the most famous castaway of all, Alexander Selkirk. In late 1703 Dampier was given charge of a gun ship, the *St George*, to battle the Spanish off the coast of South America. It set sail for Cape Horn with a smaller gunship, *Cinque Ports*, under the command of Thomas Stradling. Selkirk was the Scottish-born sailing master of *Cinque Ports*, and had himself been a buccaneer and privateer. The two ships were separated in May 1704; the *Cinque Ports* was in poor condition and the crew were sick with scurvy, and Selkirk had badly fallen out with his young captain. At Más a Tierra, an island in the Juan Fernández Archipelago, off the coast of Chile, Selkirk asked to leave the ship and be put ashore. Stradling obliged, 'denouncing the choice he had made of remaining upon the island as rank mutiny'.[33] Remarkably, Selkirk lived on Más a Tierra, alone, for over four and a half years. In 1708 Dampier helped to organise another foray against the Spanish, appointed as pilot to the gunship *Duke* under the command of Captain Woodes Rogers—another privateer who later published an account of his voyage, and would go on to become the first royal governor of the Bahamas. This voyage formed part of Dampier's third circumnavigation of the world. They arrived at Selkirk's island on 31 January 1709 and were astonished to meet the castaway. 'When he came on board the *Duke*', John Howell writes in *The Life and Adventures of Alexander Selkirk* (1829),

'Dampier gave him excellent character, telling Captain Rogers that Selkirk had been the best man on board the *Cinque Ports*. Upon this recommendation, he was immediately engaged to be mate on board the *Duke* ... Selkirk's strength and vigour were of great service to them. He caught two goats in the afternoon. They sent along with him their swiftest runners and a bulldog; but these he soon left far behind ....'[34]

Selkirk, of course, became the model for the eponymous castaway in Daniel Defoe's *The Life and Strange Surprizing Adventures of Robinson Crusoe* (1719). On a voyage to acquire African slaves in 1659, Crusoe is shipwrecked on an island in the Caribbean off the coast of Venezuela, remaining there for over twenty-seven years. The novel itself was extraordinarily popular, and initiated an often equally popular genre, the 'Robinsonade': that is, narratives about shipwrecks and castaways. Later on, we'll see examples of the Robinsonade unfolding on or around the coast of the Australian colonies. Defoe's novel wanted to present itself as true and credible, with Crusoe as its author. In some introductory remarks, an Editor insists the novel is 'a just History of Fact; neither is their [*sic*] any Appearance of Fiction in it.'[35] This is not a picaresque narrative: it claims a secure authorial voice for itself as it settles into the long haul of surviving on the island. It is often noted that Crusoe, as he resourcefully turns his environs into a habitable, homely realm ('I began to apply myself ...'), is an example of the modern liberal subject. For Franco Moretti, he is nothing less than an early incarnation of the industrious, acquisitional bourgeois.[36]

But it is just as important to note what Crusoe does both before the shipwreck and after he is finally rescued. He is already the owner of a successful plantation in Brazil, having lived there for four years. As a 'Guinea Trader', he aims to bring more African slaves to the plantations in order to 'thrive and prosper': 'And now increasing in Business and in Wealth, my Head began to be full of Projects and Undertakings beyond my Reach; such as are indeed often the Ruin of the best Heads in Business'.[37] As a castaway on the island, he plays out a similar 'story of colonial possession in the Caribbean' through his master/slave relationship with Friday.[38] The novelist James Joyce had lectured on Daniel Defoe in Trieste in 1912, famously remarking about Crusoe: 'He is the true prototype of the British colonist, as Friday (the trusty savage who arrives on an unlucky day) is the symbol of the subject races'.[39] So *Robinson Crusoe* is indeed a shipwreck and castaway adventure narrative; but it is also an account of a slave trader's ambitious claims to property and significant wealth through the subjugation, and commodification, of others.

Coming in the wake of Defoe's novel, the greatest imaginary travel adventure narrative from the eighteenth century is the Anglo–Irish writer Jonathan Swift's *Gulliver's Travels* or (in the original title) *Travels into Several Remote Nations of the World* (1726). This is another Robinsonade, with the protagonist Gulliver shipwrecked and marooned several times over in voyages that last more than sixteen years. All of his voyages are to imaginary places that are positioned in close proximity to New Holland. But it is not often noted that towards the end of Swift's satirical fantasy, Gulliver leaves the Houyhnhnms in a canoe and actually pays a visit to the Australian mainland. 'I began this desperate voyage on February 15, 1714–5, at 9 o'clock in the morning', he writes, keeping his own ship's journal. Sailing south of the Cape of Good Hope, he steers eastward, aiming 'to reach the south-west coast of New Holland'.[40] Arriving at an island off the coast, the first joke in this part of the novel is to do with cartographic inaccuracy: 'This confirmed me in the Opinion I have long entertained, that the Maps and Charts place this Country at least three Degrees more to the East than it really is ....'[41]

The account of Gulliver's experiences as he steps ashore then gently mocks Dampier's brief accounts of New Holland in his first and second journals. Dampier couldn't find fresh water; but Gulliver writes, 'I fortunately found a Brook of excellent Water, which gave me great relief'.[42] One of Dampier's crew is speared during the attack described above; referencing this event, Gulliver comes across 'twenty or thirty natives', and is wounded by an arrow that he thinks is poisoned. Commentators have often pointed out that Gulliver's ship on his first voyage into the Pacific was the *Antelope*, while the ship Dampier commanded on the voyage to New Holland was, of course, the *Roebuck*.[43] And in a letter to his cousin included in George Faulkner's 1735 edition of *Gulliver's Travels*, Gulliver claims that he advised 'my cousin Dampier' on how to publish the journal of his first voyage around the world. In the meantime, Swift's novel took the opportunity to criticise the vogue for publishing ship's journals and taking the truth of what they recorded for granted: 'I could heartily wish a law was enacted, that every traveller, before he were permitted to publish his voyages, should be obliged to make oath before the Lord High Chancellor that all he intended to print was absolutely true to the best of his knowledge ....'[44]

Truth and credibility become important to Gulliver's fantasy voyages, and he complains when a ship's captain accuses him of dreaming the whole thing. But he also wants to stress that his voyages and shipwrecks, his ramblings and meanderings, are ends in themselves, and not in the immediate service of colonial expansion. As he makes his point—and distinguishes himself from profit-seeking traders and privateers like Dampier—Gulliver gives a brief, stark account of how colonisation works that is worth quoting in full here:

> a Crew of Pyrates are driven by a Storm they know not whither, at length a Boy discovers Land from the Top-mast, they go on Shore to rob and plunder; they see an harmless People, are entertained with Kindness, they give the Country a new Name, they take formal Possession of it for their King, they set up a rotten Plank or a Stone for a Memorial, they murder two or three Dozen of the Natives, bring away a Couple more by Force for a Sample, return home, and get their Pardon. Here commences a new Dominion acquired with a Title by *Divine Right*. Ships are sent with the first Opportunity, the Natives are driven out or destroyed, their Princes tortured to discover their Gold, a free Licence given to all Acts of Inhumanity and Lust, the Earth reeking with the Blood of its Inhabitants: and this execrable Crew of Butchers employed in so pious an Expedition, is a *modern Colony* sent to convert and civilise an idolatrous and barbarous People.[45]

In this account, even pirates blown off course can end up laying the foundations for colonisation, the claiming of new territory for the king, and the killing and dispossession of Indigenous people. Disappointingly—or perhaps sarcastically, from Swift's Irish perspective?—Gulliver then identifies Britain as the exception to the rule: 'But this Description', he adds, 'doth by no means effect the British Nation, who may be an Example to the whole World for their Wisdom, Care, and Justice in planting Colonies ....'[46]

Gulliver's Travels shifts the adventure narrative to a record of imaginary voyages that both imitates and mocks records of actual voyages while making the same rhetorical claims to truth and credibility. The 'imaginary voyage' to the Global South became its own genre, with examples appearing some years before the novels of Defoe and Swift. Henry Neville's short erotic Restoration fantasy, *The Isle of Pines; or a late discovery of a fourth island, in Terra Australis Incognita* (1668), has its incestuous antihero, George Pine, shipwrecked on an imaginary 'Austral' coast with his two young daughters and two female slaves. Populating this uninhabited island with his own children ('our lust gave us liberty'), this is an early, albeit perverted, British claim on land in the South Pacific.[47] (The actual Isle of Pines is at the southern end of New Caledonia. Cook gave the island this name in 1774; 100 years later, it was used by the French as a penal colony for French criminals and revolutionaries.)

A significant number of imaginary voyages around this time saw their protagonists discovering fully-fledged European-influenced societies—'ideal Commonwealths'—already existing in Australia. Gabriel de Foigny's *Le Terre*

Australe Connue (1676) was published in English in 1693 as *A New Discovery of Terra Incognita Australis, or the Southern World, by James Sadeur, a French-man*. This strange novel presents the adventures of an orphaned ocean traveller ('conceived in *America* and brought forth upon the Ocean') who realises that he is 'of two sexes ... a Hermaphrodite'.[48] Drawing on the records of actual voyages and charts, Sadeur embarks on a journey south that sees him brave storms, shipwrecks and various fantastic obstacles to arrive naked at an Australian utopia, peopled by, it turns out, giant hermaphrodites (with both beards and breasts, etc) who live almost entirely on fruit. Sadeur cohabits with them for thirty-five years before returning to Europe; this may, incidentally, be the first literary work ever to use the term 'Australians' for its local population.

Another French 'Austral utopia' is Denis Vairasse d'Alais's *The History of the Sevarites or Sevarambi* (1675) or *Histoire des Sévarambes* (1677–79). This is a captain's memoir that imagines being shipwrecked along the coast of Australia (drawing on accounts of the notorious shipwreck of the VOC ship *Batavia* on Beacon Island in 1629) and finding a long-established population with complex social hierarchies. Hendrik Smeeks' *The Mighty Kingdom of Krinke Kesmes* (1708) is a Dutch novel coming in the wake of the Dutch exploration of what was at this time still known as New Holland. Its merchant hero sets sail for the Philippines but is driven south by a storm to a hitherto unknown kingdom that is almost an anagram of the author's name. The island once again turns out to have its own long-established population. All of these imaginary voyage novels chart the hazards of sailing into unknown regions in order to provide records of otherwise remote quasi-utopias, where Australia becomes a site for exploring alternative Euro–Asian systems of government, religion, social practice and so on. In doing so, they give us a different sense of 'adventure': that is, the adventure of gradually revealing, and getting to know, new ways of living, new ways of managing and organising human life.

The wandering global traveller became a literary trope in Europe in the eighteenth century; an expression of one's increasing capacity to move freely from one place to another, but also a tribute to one's willingness to be open-minded enough to want to *know* about those places, to be curious about them and the people who inhabit them. The key figure here is the 'citizen of the world', 'one of the programmatic, indeed fashionable phrases of the Enlightenment'.[49] An important influence on Swift's *Gulliver's Travels* was the French Huguenot writer Simon Tyssot de Patot's *The Travels and Adventures of James Massey* (1714), with its intensely curious young hero, who, early on, is inspired by a meeting with Michrob, the 'Wandering Jew': 'There is no Corner of the World but he affirm'd he had visited'.[50] The meeting, Massey tells us, 'whetted my natural Desire to travel'.[51] Appointed as a ship's surgeon (like Gulliver), he then embarks on a series of voyages, is shipwrecked, captured by pirates and sold as a slave, and marooned 'at a Place altogether unknown to us' somewhere near the East Indies. Massey and his crew remain there for eighteen years, fighting off attacks from 'savages ... all lusty, well-made fellows'.[52] Returning finally to London, much older and wiser, he insists that his record of an adventurous life should be read as an intellectual exercise rather than used as a handbook for subsequent colonial domination: 'I was afraid ... my Book would excite the Ambition of some insatiable Monarch to conquer the Kingdom I describe; and that he would compel me to serve as a Guide to those who should be employ'd in so difficult an Expedition. But, alas! I am weary of travelling, and too old to bear the Fatigues which I have endur'd heretofore'.[53]

John Hawkesworth's 1773 publication of the journals of James Cook and Joseph Banks (alongside the journals of other commanders, such as John Byron) significantly changed the nature of voyage narratives about New Holland and the South Pacific, not least by enabling the spirit of the Enlightenment and the imperative for colonial domination to go hand in hand. Hawkesworth's Preface might seem designed precisely to 'excite the ambitions' of the monarch, George III, addressing him directly:

> Sir,
>
> After the great improvements that have been made in Navigation since the discovery of America, it may well be thought strange that a very considerable part of the globe on which we live should still have remained unknown; that it should still have been the subject of speculation ... But the cause has probably been, that sovereign Princes have seldom any motive for attempting the discovery of new countries than to conquer them, that the advantages of conquering new countries which

> must first be discovered are remote and uncertain, and that ambition has always found objects nearer home.[54]

This is a passage about colonisation as a matter of speculation and risk; interestingly, it seems to suggest, against the grain of an expansive program of empire building, that the risks of colonising remote places can sometimes overshadow the advantages. Hawkesworth continues, sounding a little like Gulliver, who had condemned the harsh brutalities of colonisation but invoked Britain as a kind of enlightened exception to the general rule:

> It is the distinguishing characteristic of Your Majesty to act from more liberal motives; and having the best fleet, and the bravest as well as most able navigators in Europe, Your Majesty has, not with a view to the acquisition of treasure, or the extent of dominion, but the improvement of commerce and the increase and diffusion of knowledge, undertaken what has so long been neglected; and under Your Majesty's auspices, in little more than seven years, discoveries have been made far greater than those of all the navigators in the world collectively, from the expedition of Columbus to the present time.[55]

The 'improvement of commerce', and the 'increase and diffusion of knowledge': these are the nobler (or pragmatic) imperatives of an empire's adventure narrative that can mask the brutal fact of colonisation itself. Two imaginary colonial adventure novels came in the wake of Hawkesworth's journal as well as the journals associated with Cook's second voyage around the world. The first was the anonymous *The Travels of Hildebrand Bowman* (1778), dedicated to two of the naturalists who had sailed with Cook, Joseph Banks and Daniel Solander.[56] 'Gentlemen', Bowman writes,

> I address these *Travels* to you, as the best judges of the veracity of some part of them ... Should Government think proper to send any ships to cultivate friendship and commerce with the Nations I have discovered, and I am honoured with the command of one of them, nothing could add so much to my satisfaction on that event, as the company of two Gentlemen, who have set so laudable an example to all the European Literati, of braving the greatest dangers in the pursuit of useful knowledge.[57]

Colonisation has no role to play in this early account, although it is doubtful that the novel itself delivers anything much to do with 'useful knowledge'. Bowman grows up 'reading books of Voyages and Travels, whenever I could meet with them'; inspired by stories about 'Captain Cooke's [*sic*] voyage around the world in the *Endeavour* bark', he enlists in the navy.[58] The novel follows Cook's second voyage when Bowman is appointed as a midshipman on Tobias Furneaux's *Adventure*, which sailed with Cook's *Resolution* in 1772. We have already noted that the *Adventure* was separated from the *Resolution* during the voyage, having been blown off course. In late 1773 it arrived at Queen Charlotte Sound on the northern tip of New Zealand's South Island. Putting ashore at a place Cook had previously named Grass Cove, Bowman goes hunting in the forests. When he returns to his ten companions, he finds them all killed, their bodies surrounded by 'natives'. This scene is based on an actual event, described by the *Resolution*'s George Forster in his own voyage journal, also mentioned earlier. The *Adventure*, Forster writes, had sent a boat to Grass Cove 'in order to gather a load of celery and scurvy-grass for the crew'.[59] The boat's commander, Mr Rowe, 'look[ed] upon all the natives of the South Sea with contempt', encouraging his crew to shoot at nearby *Māori* ('till all their ammunition was spent') when one of the sailor's jackets was stolen. In retaliation, the *Māori* then 'killed every one of them'. The event became notorious for a number of reasons, not least because it seemed to involve subsequent acts of cannibalism; Forster himself thought that Europeans committed far greater atrocities.[60]

The Grass Cove killings function as a trigger that catapults Bowman's narrative into pure fantasy. Left alone, he becomes a castaway and eventually rows to the North Island. *The Travels of Hildebrand Bowman* is sometimes regarded as New Zealand's first novel; but, no doubt traumatised by his landfall experience there, Bowman erases any actual presence of *Māori* people, writing instead about the Carnovirrians, a violent and cannibalistic tribe of people who are placed at a distance in the narrative, threatening but remote. He makes his way instead towards a series of well-established societies, each defined by a particular trait: the inhabitants of Olfactaria have a heightened sense of smell and value good hygiene, the Auditante locals have excellent hearing and enjoy good music, and so on. These all turn out to be recognisable versions of European social and political life—'ideal Commonwealths'—that allow him (in most cases) to feel more or less at home. He gives them advice and helps them to advance their technologies; these societies may be familiar in most respects but Bowman still needs to demonstrate European superiority. Swift's *Gulliver's Travels* is clearly an influence here, except that Bowman is a commercial trader and speculator who also aims to exploit every opportunity available to him wherever he goes. 'How surprising it is to me, who am of a trading nation', he writes, 'to learn, that there are people on the other side of the globe, who have carried navigation to such a height, as to send ships all over the face of the earth ....'[61] It is as if Europe sees itself reflected here in an oddly exaggerated mirror. He finally leaves New Zealand on a Dutch ship from Batavia, whose captain believes 'there was no civilised nation in that part of the globe'.[62] Bowman thinks differently; he imagines that he has in fact discovered the mythical great southern land, which, in a massive act of (deluded) ego, he names Bowmania.

The First Fleet brought colonisation to Australia in January 1788, establishing a penal and military settlement at Warrane/Sydney Cove under Governor Arthur Phillip. The first novel to take its characters out to this actually existing (as opposed to imaginary) Australian colony was a German narrative serialised in a women's magazine in 1793–94 and published in 1801: Therese Huber's *Abentheuer auf einer Reise nach Neu-Holland*, or *Adventures on a Journey to New Holland*. Huber was 'one of the first professional women writers of German literature', although much of her work around this time was published in her husband's name (Ludwig Ferdinand Huber).[63] Some years earlier, she had in fact been married to George Forster. She was familiar not only with her estranged husband's voyage journal but also the journals of Cook and, most probably, the journals of First Fleet crew such as Watkin Tench, John White and Arthur Phillip himself, all of which had appeared in German editions by the early 1790s.

Her protagonist, Rudolph, is supposed to be based on Forster, but his journey and experiences are vastly different in kind. Fleeing revolutionary France, Rudolph finds himself on a women's convict ship heading to New South Wales: this is a long way from Forster's journey of exploration on Cook's *Resolution*. In his letters home, Rudolph regards himself as 'a citizen of the world, rejected by every well-ordered community': he belongs everywhere, and nowhere.[64] On board the convict ship, he tries to teach himself Arabic, thinking of other random future destinations. He meets Mr Sidney, a surgeon who is tending to a sickly convict woman, Frances Belton, transported for killing a man who had tried to rape her. Later, Frances helps to deliver another convict's child, adopting the infant when the woman dies. Rudolph demonises the female convicts on the ship ('those monstrous creatures') but, along with Sidney, he comes to venerate Frances. The two men soon fall in love with her.

At Warrane/Sydney Cove, Rudolph unleashes his contempt for convicts, thinking they are irredeemable. The colony, he writes, is a 'natural paradise' but 'a lamentable race of men disfigures it. They lack every impulse to be virtuous'.[65] Frances gets respectable work as a housekeeper, but Rudolph leaves the colony almost immediately, sailing to Norfolk Island. George Forster and Cook had arrived at Norfolk Island in October

1774; in his voyage journal, Forster called it a 'pretty little spot'.[66] Arthur Phillip had sent convicts and some free men to the island soon after the arrival of the First Fleet; it later became a penal settlement (see Chapter 2) and a site for agriculture. In Huber's novel, the east coast of New Holland can be seen from the island, which is now well cultivated, with hedgerows, little houses and so on. Rudolph calls it 'the paradise of this region'.[67] It turns out that Frances's long-lost husband, Henry—also a transported convict, a morally righteous political rebel—is already living on Norfolk Island. Soon the couple are reunited, Frances is declared innocent, and so distinguished from the other convicts ('the dregs of society'), and both Rudolph and Sidney, dejected, take the next available ship to India. 'In the company of my love-stricken young friend', he writes, 'I shall roam over other Oceans and other Continents ... a homeless exile'.[68]

The Travels of Hildebrand Bowman presents a traumatic encounter with New Zealand *Māori* and then places them at a distance, in order to populate the country with a series of imaginary European-like societies defined primarily by the role they play in global trade. Huber's novel doesn't see Aboriginal people at all and has nothing to say about colonisation. New Holland, for Rudolph, is a *terra nullius*, like Norfolk Island—which is where the novel prefers to be. Here, it can work through its sentimental vision of what Lisa O'Connell calls 'a remote and privatised domestic scene',[69] far away from the turmoil of Europe but also untouched by the colony itself, which the novel imagines as utterly debased. Huber's protagonists float free of colonisation, even as they arrive in its aftermath.

They are not involved in commercial trade and, although he collects a few plants (in a brief nod to Forster, who collected numerous botanical specimens during his voyage with Cook), Rudolph does not have any scientific curiosity. Leaving Norfolk Island broken-hearted, he 'passed through China, wandered aimlessly in India and crossed the Arabian Sea to Egypt from where the most unexplored portion of the earth beckoned to him'.[70] He dies alone, a 'stranger' everywhere—although not in Simmel's sense of the word. This adventure novel refuses to allow its protagonist to settle in any place, moving him randomly from one country to another. He is constantly leaving and going somewhere else. Lifting Rudolph out of the project of colonisation altogether—even as it draws on some of colonisation's foundational texts—the novel's focus is instead on global wandering as an entirely aimless activity, without end.

CHAPTER 2

Transportation and Convict Adventures

When the First Fleet sailed into Port Jackson on Eora Country in January 1788, it brought with it around 750 convicts on board six of its eleven ships. During the early years of colonisation, there were often more convicts than settlers among the non-Aboriginal population of New South Wales. John Dunmore Lang was Warrane/Sydney's first Presbyterian minister and a radical republican; the colonies, he dryly noted in 1837, are 'almost exclusively colonies of convicts'.[1] Lang wasn't opposed to convict transportation as such, but he did speak up for a more humane system of colonial punishment that aimed to encourage convicts to reform and assimilate into settler society. He was partly arguing with Richard Whately, the Catholic archbishop of Dublin, who in 1834 had written influentially about transportation as a 'method of colonisation' that was doomed to fail (as it had earlier on in the United States) because it 'pours into the country they wish to colonise, a population who would not, perhaps, of themselves, gone there'—and who would consequently regard Britain itself as an 'odious' place to which they could no longer owe any loyalty.[2] For the republican Lang, however, this was a good thing, an opportunity to bring convicts into the service of the colonies themselves. Transportation as a punishment was meant to be better than death, not worse. Humane treatment could mean that convicts had something to look forward to at the end of a long, arduous and exhausting voyage. But when they arrived, they needed to be put to work. Convicts were an unpaid labour force, conscripted by law into the raw business of colonisation: building roads and houses, clearing forests, planting crops, extracting minerals and so on. For Lang, convicts were therefore an excellent colonial investment, so long as they were treated well; that is, well enough to be able to do hard labour outside in often harsh conditions without wanting to abscond. 'Under a proper system of management', he wrote (thinking purely in terms of profit), 'the labour of a convict at a penal settlement might be made to produce on the Australian continent double, triple, or even four times the whole cost of his maintenance'.[3]

Naturally, the convicts themselves didn't always see things this way. The very first issue of the first newspaper in the colonies, the *Sydney Gazette and New South Wales Advertiser*, was published on 5 March 1803. It reported that fifteen Irish convict labourers had absconded from Castle Hill Government Farm, raiding settlers' properties and committing 'many acts of violence and atrocity'.[4] A few years later, in June 1806, the *Sydney Gazette* remarked on the discovery of the remains of one of these escapees:

> Last week a native informed Tarlington, a settler, that the skeleton of a white man, with a musket and tin kettle laying beside him, had been seen under the first ridge of the mountains. The settler accompanied the native, and found the skeleton, &c., as described; the bones of which being very long, leads to a more than probable conjecture, that the remains are those of James Hughes, who absconded from Castle Hill the 15th of February, 1803, in company with 15 others, most of whom had recently arrived in the *Hercules*, on the ridiculous pretext of finding a road to China, but in reality to commit the most unheard of depradations [*sic*]: the consequences of which were, that the whole except Hughes were shortly apprehended, and 13 capitally convicted before a Criminal Court, of whom two were executed, and 11 pardoned.[5]

The newspaper took the opportunity to use Hughes's death as a cautionary tale for other convicts who might also have been thinking of escaping from the colony: 'it is hoped his miserable end will warn the thoughtless, inexperienced and depraved against an inclination to exchange the comfort and security derived from honest labour; to depart from which can only lead to the most fatal consequences'.[6] This is essentially a warning against the possibility of any kind of convict adventure.

Convict transportation by ship from England was part of a sequence of incarcerations that would often begin on a local prison hulk (usually, decommissioned naval vessels) at a port such as Woolwich or Plymouth. Charles Dickens's novel *Great Expectations* (1862) begins somewhere around 1807, with the convict Abel Magwitch—'a great iron on his leg'—escaping from a prison hulk on the Thames estuary.[7] Chains and shackles were used on convict ships, too, where conditions could indeed be grim. The Second Fleet arrived at Warrane/Sydney Cove in June 1790; some of its convict ships were contracted to agents involved in the slave trade, and the treatment of convicts on board was so harsh that over 250 men and eleven women died during the voyage.[8] Captain William Hill, who sailed on the *Surprize*, wrote that 'The slave trade is merciful compared with what I have seen on this fleet'—where convicts could be shackled in such a way that it was 'impossible for them to move but at the risk of both legs being broken'.[9]

Commentators noted at the time the close parallels between the enslavement of Africans in the New World and the colonies' treatment of the 'English felon'.[10] Arthur Phillip, the first governor of New South Wales, had famously said, 'There *can be no slavery in a free land and consequently no slaves*'.[11] But the treatment of convicts on the Second Fleet in particular would suggest otherwise: that 'the categories of Australian convict and African slave overlapped considerably'.[12] Given the sheer brutality they were exposed to, escaping from the colony on arrival (if one survived the journey) was at the very least an attempt to recover some level of agency and self-determination in a system designed to completely negate these things. It was also an expression of one's refusal to invest in the entire colonial enterprise—to reject any form of participation (including hard labour) in the colony's nation-building plans and aspirations. This is all a long way from John Dunmore Lang. The idea was to get as far away from the colony as possible, as soon as you could. The warnings of the *Sydney Gazette* notwithstanding, this is where the great convict adventure begins.

As with James Hughes above, China was for a while a preferred, if often imaginary, destination. Watkin Tench was a naval officer who sailed with the First Fleet on the convict ship *Charlotte*; he went on to publish extensive records of early colonial life, to great acclaim. In *A Complete Account of the Settlement at Port Jackson, in New South Wales* (1793), Tench recorded an early convict escape, in November 1791, from the farming settlement of Rose Hill (by this time, also known as Parramatta):

> A very extraordinary instance of folly stimulated to desperation, occurred in the beginning of this month, among the convicts at Rose Hill. Twenty men, and a pregnant woman, part of those who had arrived in the last fleet, suddenly disappeared with their clothes, working tools, bedding, and their provisions ... The first intelligence heard of them, was from some convict settlers, who said they had seen them pass, and enquired whither they were bound. To which they had received for an answer, 'to *China*'. The extravagance and infatuation of such an attempt was explained to them, by the settlers; but neither derision, nor demonstration, could avert them from pursuing their purpose.[13]

It would have been unusual to associate convicts with 'extravagance'. Mostly, as they served out their sentences, their lives would have been austere, heavily disciplined, and pretty much worn down. Soon afterwards, Tench visited a makeshift hospital at Parramatta and talked to four of the '*Chinese travellers*', who had been attacked and wounded as they made their way across land occupied by Dharug (Burramattagal) people:

> I asked these men if they really supposed it possible to reach China; they answered, that they were certainly made to believe (they knew not how) that at a considerable distance to the northward existed a large river, which separated this country from the back part of China; and that when it should be crossed (which was practicable) they would find themselves among a copper-coloured people, who would receive and treat them kindly: they added, that on the third day of their elopement, one of the party died of fatigue; another they saw butchered by the natives, who, finding them unarmed, attacked them and put them to flight. This happened near Broken Bay, which harbour stopped their progress to the northward, and forced them to turn to the right hand, by which means they soon after found themselves on the sea shore, where they wandered about, in a destitute condition, picking up shell fish to allay hunger ... On their road back they met six fresh adventurers, sallying forth to join them ...[14]

Even as these defeated convicts made their way back to the colony, other 'fresh adventurers', it seems, were already embarking on the same long, hazardous journey—with China working here not so much as an actual destination but, rather, as a kind of ideal, an aspiration.[15]

The New South Wales governor, John Hunter, wrote to the Duke of Portland in February 1798, 'I have now to inform your Grace of a far more numerous gang, who had provided what they thought necessary for their expedition ... and were furnished with a paper of written instructions how they were to travel in point of direction from hence ... to China'.[16] This particular convict ambition seems to have played itself out many times over in the early moments of colonisation. The inveterate Irish thief and pickpocket George Barrington was transported to New South Wales on the *Active*, one of a number of convict ships to sail with the Third Fleet, arriving in September 1791. He received a conditional pardon a year later and went on to become Parramatta's chief constable. Published under his name (although he was almost certainly not its author), *The History of New South Wales, including Botany Bay, Port Jackson, Parramatta, Sydney, and All its Dependencies* (1802) provides many examples of convict attempts to escape the colony and travel to China: a 'party of convicts' from Parramatta, who, not long after the Third Fleet arrived, sought 'a passage to China'; an Irish convict who spent 'several days in search of a road which was to have conducted him to China, or the new ideal colony of white people'; later on, some Irish convicts 'who had for some time been searching for a road to China', and so on.[17] To give yet another example: John Place and two other convicts were working at Castle Hill in May 1803 (around the same time those fifteen Irish convicts mentioned above had absconded, raiding settler properties). The *Sydney Gazette* told his 'melancholy' story the following month, reporting that Place and his companions had decided 'to get to China, by which means they would obtain their liberty again.'[18] But the companions are reported to have died in the bush; Place, exhausted by the journey, was found by a settler who was hunting with Dharug people for kangaroos; and the newspaper ends its report by berating him for his 'ignorance' and 'delusion'.

Benjamin Mountford has commented on John Place's attempted escape in *Britain, China, and Colonial Australia* (2016), where he suggests that some absconding convicts—by stowing away, for example—might have actually reached their destination, not least because convict ships, after arriving in the colonies, often headed off to China on trading missions.[19] The word *abscond* means 'to depart suddenly and secretly', usually to escape payment of a debt or some other legal obligation. It comes from the Latin *abscondere*, to hide or conceal or put out of sight; or even to store or stow away. The absconding convict might in fact end up almost anywhere and the journeys they embarked upon could be epic in scale. The greatest and most ambitious early convict escape involved a number of convicts who had been transported with the First Fleet in 1788 on the same ship as Watkin Tench, the *Charlotte*. Mary Broad came from Cornwall, and had been transported for robbing and assaulting a woman in Plymouth. On board the convict ship, she met her future husband, William Bryant, a Cornish fisherman. She was already pregnant at this time and gave birth to a daughter (named Charlotte) off the coast of Rio de Janeiro. James Martin, a bricklayer, was also on the *Charlotte*; so was a carpenter, James Cox. Bryant was 'placed in charge of managing the colony's fishing enterprise', but as Tim Causer notes, a flogging in February 1789, along with the arrival in Warrane/ Sydney of so many sick and maltreated convicts on the Second Fleet, may have influenced his decision to abscond.[20]

With the aim of seizing a boat, Bryant set about gathering a crew: his wife Mary, along with Martin and Cox from the *Charlotte*, Samuel Bird from the *Alexander* (also from the First Fleet), and four convicts from the Second Fleet—the mariner William Allen; Samuel Broom; a weaver, Nathaniel Lillie; and William Morton, another experienced mariner. Causer describes the 'extraordinary degree of preparation' these convicts went to as they made plans for what they hoped would be a journey that would take them as far away from the colony as they could get.[21] Around the end of March 1791, the convicts stole the colony's six-oar fishing boat and, along with Mary's two young children (a son, Emanuel, was born in April 1790), rowed out of Warrane/Sydney Cove. Watkin Tench described the escape in his 1793 chronicle of settlement at Port Jackson, expressing his admiration for the convicts' sheer resolve:

> They seized the governor's cutter; and putting into her a seine [fishing net], fishing lines, and hooks, fire-arms, a quadrant, compass, and some provisions, boldly pushed out to sea, determined to brave every danger, and combat every hardship, rather than remain in a captive state ... Among them were a fisherman, a carpenter, and some competent navigators; so that little doubt was entertained, that a scheme so admirably planned, would be admirably executed.[22]

The nine convicts and the two children arrived in Kupang (Coupang) in West Timor ten weeks later on 5 June 1791, having travelled around 5000 kilometres.

The nature and trajectory of this remarkable voyage recall the notorious mutiny just two years earlier on William Bligh's *Bounty*, with Bligh and eighteen crew put into a 23-foot boat not far from Tofua, east of Fiji, carrying enough provisions for about five days. They, too, sailed to Timor, arriving at Kupang on 14 June 1789. Bryant would have known about Bligh's voyage in an open boat, and no doubt took some inspiration from it. The Dutch governor at Kupang treated the convicts well at first, believing Bryant's story that they were from a foundered whaling ship; but, later, hearing that they were absconders, he put them in prison. They were then sent to Batavia and clasped in irons on a hulk. William Bryant and his infant son both died there. Cox, Bird and Morton died on the way to the Cape of Good Hope. The remaining convicts, including James Martin and Mary Bryant, were placed on board the HMS *Gorgon*, one of the ships in the Third Fleet, and taken back to England.

Coincidentally, Watkin Tench was also on this ship and wrote once again about the absconders, feeling a close bond with Bryant, in particular. 'I confess that I never looked at these people, without pity and astonishment', he wrote. 'They had miscarried in a heroic struggle for liberty; after having combated every hardship, and conquered every difficulty'.[23] Bryant's daughter Charlotte died in this part of the voyage. We should note that her death, her brother's death and the death of four of the convicts occurred not during the epic escape in an open boat, but in British custody later on. It was a risk to arrive back in England: a transported convict returning home, like Magwitch in Dickens's novel, could face arrest, imprisonment, trial and possibly execution. The absconders were sent to Newgate Prison, but, as Causer notes, the renowned Scottish lawyer and biographer James Boswell took an interest in their case and came to their aid. Mary Bryant was pardoned in May 1793 and Boswell regularly sent her money. The other convicts were pardoned six months later, in November.

While in Newgate Prison, James Martin wrote an account of his escape with Mary Bryant and the others, titled *Memorandoms*. The manuscript was first discovered by Charles Blount in the mid-1930s, among the papers of the political and economic philosopher Jeremy Bentham, held at University College, London (UCL). Bentham was a critic of convict transportation to New South Wales—his writings on this topic influenced Richard Whately—and was also heavily invested in 'progressive' forms of prison design, offering his 'panopticon penitentiary scheme' to the British government around the time Martin and the others were planning to seize a fishing boat and abscond from the colony.[24] The most recent edition of Martin's *Memorandoms* was edited and introduced by Tim Causer, and published by UCL Press in 2017; it is freely available online. We have seen examples of a captain's ship journal in Chapter 1. Martin's account is a convict absconder's open boat journal, but as an adventure narrative it shares some recognisable generic features with its grander, more official cousin. There are a number of encounters with Aboriginal people as the convicts sail north along the Australian coast; some are friendly and some seem threatening, with chases in canoes and some close calls ('there Came they natives in Varse Numbers with Spears & Shields').[25] There are heavy storms, and the boat is occasionally blown off course. The convicts worry about getting shipwrecked, the boat often filling with water. They become castaways for a week or so, marooned on an uninhabited island off the Queensland coast (probably Lady Elliot Island), where they survive by eating turtles and birds. There is great relief when they finally arrive at West Timor, but Martin blames William Bryant for informing on them and landing them in prison. They are taken to the Cape of Good Hope with some of the 'Bounty Pirates', who had also been rounded up by the British. 'We were all glad we had not perished at sea', Martin writes as this epic journey finally comes to an end, just before they are met in England by police constables, taken before a magistrate and 'fully committed to Newgate'.[26]

In *The Road to Botany Bay* (1987), Paul Carter suggested that a convict's understanding of China as a place well beyond 'the bounds of the penal colony' was a 'figure of speech' (they didn't always know where it was or how to get there), even as it made escape itself 'conceivable'.[27] But China was by no means the only trigger here. Absconding convicts were stirred into action by the possibility of a range of destinations, right across the Asia-Pacific Rim and further afield. Grace Karskens has spoken up for 'the extraordinary feats of daring, courage and resilience by ordinary people whose names we often do not even know' in the early years of colonial history, when there were at least seventy convict escapes from Botany Bay and Norfolk Island between 1788 and 1810, and possibly 'many more' unaccounted for.[28] Convict absconders might walk (or sail as stowaways) towards China, but they might also go inland and head west; they might sail for Timor, as the Bryants and their companions had done; they might head to India or Japan; or they might travel by ship across the Pacific to New Zealand or towards South America. Many were recaptured, brought back to the colony and punished, even executed, while others may indeed have made new lives for themselves elsewhere. But they are all people who, sentenced to be shipped out to the colonies and put to work, refused to participate in transportation and incarceration as a 'method of colonisation' (to recall Whately).

Seizing ships—as opposed to open boats—gave convicts real capacity to head out to their destinations with greater precision and better infrastructures of support. Ian Duffield has talked about 'convict piracy', which began with attempted mutinies on board transport ships. He notes the convict seizure of over eighty ships in the Australian colonies between 1790 and 1829, and reads these as determinedly rational, quasi-revolutionary acts; 'aboard a newly pirated vessel', he writes, convicts 'enacted liberty by literally and symbolically deciding their course and destination'.[29] Duffield goes on to talk about an 'Indian and Pacific Ocean diaspora of convict sea-escapers' who, when they did manage to settle in some place far away from the colonies, effectively created 'geographies of disconnection' from the scope and imperatives of empire.[30]

We can see a striking example of this in a first-hand account of convict piracy from the early 1830s that became an important source text for the best-known convict novel from the colonial period, Marcus Clarke's *His Natural Life* (1874)—which we will discuss below. James Porter was one of a number of convicts who, in January 1834, seized the *Frederick*, a brig that had been left at Parralaongatek/Macquarie Harbour, on the west coast of lutruwita/Tasmania, when the penal settlement there was being closed down and convicts were being evacuated. Porter's chronicle of his subsequent adventures was published in the government printer James Ross's *Hobart Town Almanack and Van Diemen's Land Annual* in 1838, while the manuscript of the longer *Autobiography of Convict James Porter, Written on Norfolk Island, 1840-1844* is held at the State Library of New South Wales. Born near London, Porter went to sea early on, travelling widely but often objecting to the cruelty of his commanders. In about 1820 he went ashore at Valparaíso in Chile, a bustling trading port and major stopover for merchant ships in the Pacific. There he married a local woman, Catalina, and they had a child. But Porter was restless: 'I again (like Gulliver)', he writes, 'felt an inclination to go to sea for a trip or two and I mentioned it to my wife which gave her great uneasiness'.[31] This is a familiar refrain in a man's seafaring adventure narrative: men leave and travel long distances, women remain at home. Returning to England, Porter is later arrested for stealing, sent to a prison hulk at Woolwich, and eventually transported to Van Diemen's Land on the convict ship *Asia I*, arriving there in January 1824.

These were the early years of the Tasmanian War, and Porter, gaining some trust from the authorities, was sent on an inland expedition, where he was involved in violent exchanges with palawa people. So here, he served the interests of the colony. But he came under suspicion and was sent to work on a chain gang.

Porter decided to seize a boat and gathered a crew together, but was pursued and hid in the bush. Caught and arrested, he was placed on a ship but jumped over the side: this is a convict who was literally not on board with the project of colonisation. He was caught again and sent to Macquarie Harbour with '200 miserable beings', enduring 'misery, flogging and starvation'.[32]

The Macquarie Harbour penal settlement had been operating since 1822 and had a reputation as the harshest penitentiary in the colonies. When it closed down a little over ten years later, the *Frederick* was left behind. Porter and nine other convicts seized the brig, putting the captain and crew into a boat, and allowing them to depart with a share of the provisions. As they sailed off, William Shiers (or Shires), a carpenter, told the captain, 'we only want our liberty'; the convict John Barker took command of the ship, telling the others, 'I can navigate around the world'.[33] They sailed south of New Zealand and crossed the Pacific, heading for Chile and finally making landfall in a leaking ship that was beginning to sink. For a while, they saw no inhabitants and it seemed as if they were castaways. But they made their way to Valdivia, about 1000 kilometres south of the Chilean port where, more than a decade earlier, Porter had met his wife. A sympathetic Spanish governor allowed them to work and mix with the local population, but they were placed under guard for their own protection in February 1835, when a British frigate, HMS *Blonde*, under the command of Francis Mason, came looking for them. The great naturalist Charles Darwin was in Valdivia during this time, coincidentally; he recorded a major earthquake (20 February 1835), which for some reason Porter never mentions.[34] A few months later, a new governor arrived in Valdivia—a 'Tyrant'—who was far more hostile to the convicts. Getting permission to build a boat for official use, they planned another escape; but four were left behind, including Porter, and as punishment were confined for seven months in a cell, 'Chained two and two like dogs'.[35] The *Blonde* finally returned to claim them; they were put on the *Leviathan* hulk and eventually shipped back on the *Sarah* to Van Diemen's Land, where they expected to be hanged.

Porter's *Hobart Town Almanac* account was written in Hobart Gaol in 1837, but his *Autobiography* continues the narrative into the early 1840s. He remained in prison for more than two years, and was then transported to Norfolk Island, which, in 1839, was administered by another 'Tyrant', 'Major Bumbry' (actually, Thomas Bunbury). Porter's life was especially miserable here. But in March 1840 Bunbury was replaced by the Scottish-born Alexander Maconochie—a prison reformer influenced by the writings of Richard Whately, among others, although, like Dunmore Lang, he wasn't against transportation as such. The previous year, Maconochie had published *Australiana: Thoughts on Convict Management*, where he argued against severe physical punishments and 'coerced, or Slave labour' in the penal colonies, recommending instead a system of 'moral influence' where prisoners could earn 'marks of commendation'.[36] His arrival at Norfolk Island had an almost immediate effect on Porter: 'we have given our words neither to abscond with a boat', he writes,

> or allow one to be taken under any Circumstances and we have proved to him and all the officers on the island

> that our Commandant's Humanity [h]as brought us to a sense of our duty never to lose the only thing an unfortunate doth possess—His Word ... thus you find my gentle reader after all my trials and troubles I am now at Norfolk island and live in hopes by my good conduct to become once more a member of good Society.[37]

This is the end of Porter's *Autobiography*, which sees the literal *re-forming* of a convict pirate and serial absconder, who—back on board at last—finally commits himself to the protocols of good (unadventurous) colonial citizenship.

Transportation could itself produce adventure narratives, taking people far away from home, and presenting an often-challenging range of obstacles and encounters along the way. *The Life, and Surprising Adventures of Blue-eyed Patty*—a chapbook published anonymously some time in the 1790s—is a title that parodically echoes Defoe's much earlier *The Life and Strange Surprizing Adventures of Robinson Crusoe.* The narrative itself, however, could not be more different. Patty Freelove, the daughter of a wealthy Essex farmer, is bullied by her stepmother and deeply in love with a neighbour's son, Charles. When Charles is sentenced to be transported for poaching, Patty disguises herself as a man and secretly boards the convict ship to be with him. Off the coast of Rio de Janeiro, she has a close encounter with a shark. Later, she rejects the amorous advances of a 'Portuguese Lady', who then hires some ruffians to molest her; but Charles chases them away. At Port Jackson, they are attacked by Eora people, 'armed with spears and arrows'.[38] Patty is speared in the chest and her gender is discovered when she is attended to; when she recovers, she marries Charles and, with Governor Arthur Phillip's permission, they return to England. This short narrative ends by noting some significant events in the colony, including the 'payback' spearing of Arthur Phillip himself (on 7 September 1790) by an Eora man at Kai'ymay/Manly Cove—an event the narrative echoes with Patty, who, even as a visitor in this otherwise light-hearted adventure/romp, is still subjected to the violence of a colonial encounter. A later pamphlet, Sophie Edwards's *Surprising Misfortunes of Sophia Johnson* (1838), gives us another adventurous cross-dressing woman who similarly attempts to get from England to the colonies to be reunited with her transported lover. She sails in September 1830 'in man's apparel', as Patty had done.[39] There is a terrible storm; she is marooned, alone and desolate, on an island; but three days later, she is rescued by a Dutch merchant ship and taken to Amsterdam. It takes a couple of years for Sophia to finally get to New South Wales, where she meets her lover at last, gets married and returns with him to England to live 'in the greatest harmony'.[40]

In these boisterous cross-dressing women's adventures, a man's crime in England, his transportation to the colonies and possibly colonisation itself are all obstacles to a romantic conclusion that ends back where it began. Margaret Catchpole was a house servant and cook from Suffolk, and a skilled horsewoman. In May 1797 she was convicted of stealing a horse from John Cobbold—while dressed as a man—and was sentenced to be transported for seven years. Languishing in Ipswich Gaol, she escaped in March 1800 disguised as a sailor, was recaptured, and then sentenced again, this time to be transported for life. Catchpole was placed on the *Nile* with ninety-five other female prisoners and four convict children, arriving at Warrane/Sydney Cove on 14 December 1801.

Richard Cobbold was John Cobbold's youngest son, a Suffolk clergyman. His *The History of Margaret Catchpole* (1845)—published in the United States as *The History and Extraordinary Adventures of Margaret Catchpole* (1846)—is a moralising novel about Catchpole's life that admires her spirit but regards her as a victim of 'error' and misjudgement. Her lover in England, Will Laud, is an ambitious smuggler and sailor; 'He should go round the world', one of his crew says, and they jokingly call him 'Captain Cook'.[41] Catchpole is 'at the mercy of dangerous passions' and deeply attached to Laud.[42] Imprisoned himself, he later helps her to escape but they are both soon caught again and are transported to New South Wales. Warrane/Sydney, Catchpole thinks, 'is like a place of demons'; she doesn't much like Aboriginal people but she has some Christian sympathy for convicts, who seem 'left without instruction'.[43] She works for a while at Governor King's Female Orphan Asylum, but then meets a virtuous English farmer, John Barry, whom she marries, living along Dyarubbin/the Hawkesbury River. 'The free settlers are the great farmers of this country', she says, enthusiastically. Widowed later on, she moves back to Warrane/Sydney and is known in the colony for 'the unostentatious character of her habits of life'.[44] Cobbald's narrative turns out to be the opposite of so many convict adventures. Far from being a place where Catchpole's adventurous spirit is unleashed, the colony works instead to restrain and diminish her, overseeing her transition from horse stealer and convict to a good, dutiful settler, with nothing much left, finally, to tell about her life.

In colonial writing, the transportation romance was an identifiable genre and could sometimes be just one component of a larger adventure narrative that, in some cases, would take its characters around the world. John Nicol was born in Currie, on the outskirts of Edinburgh, in 1755. He grew up witnessing 'the dispersal of my father's family' as his siblings headed off to the Caribbean and the Americas.[45] Like so many of the young men in early adventure narratives, he soon goes to sea, travelling to Greenland, Canada, the Caribbean, Granada (where he is disgusted by the slave trade), South America, the Pacific (visiting 'the island where Captain Cook was killed'), and China, where he is 'engaged to take home a cargo of tea for the East India Company'.[46] He charts his various voyages in his memoir, *The Life and Adventures of John Nicol* (1822), recorded and edited by the Scottish inventor and bookbinder John Howell—who, as we noted in Chapter 1, went on to write *The Life and Adventures of Alexander Selkirk* (1829). Nicol tells us that he eventually returned to Scotland in 1788, planning to settle down. But a letter from his ship's captain 'rekindled my wandering propensities with as great vigour as ever', and he is appointed as a steward on the *Lady Juliana*, a transport ship that sailed from Plymouth with around 240 female convicts in July 1789.[47]

Nicol's *Life and Adventures* is one of the few written records of this voyage. The ship arrived in Warrane/Sydney

Cove in early June 1790, with four convicts escaping at the beginning of the journey, and five deaths along the way; a relatively low number at this time. Nicol has a lot of sympathy for the convict women, but happily participates in sexual relations on board a ship that recently came to be known (thanks to a 2006 account of the voyage by the Cornish-born historian Siân Rees, and Mark Lewis's film dramatisation the same year) as 'the floating brothel'. This is Nicol's account, which seems frank enough about his own involvement here: 'every man on board took a wife from among the convicts, they nothing loath. The girl with whom I lived, for I was as bad in this point as the others, was named Sarah Whitlam'.[48] In fact, he falls in love, and Sarah gives birth to a child shortly before they arrive at the colony. But in Warranc/Sydney, he loses touch with her and is later dismayed to hear she has sailed to Bombay (Mumbai). 'Unconstant woman!', he complains; he never sees her or the son again.[49] Transportation can provide a romantic interlude in a wandering life, but in this case it doesn't last long—and it raises a question that probably can't be answered here: why did Sarah leave, taking her child with her? Nicol leaves the colony as well, and —perhaps like Sarah?—becomes a global traveller. He works on a Pacific whaler, fights in the French Revolutionary Wars and, on the *Goliath*, the Battle of the Nile, and trades and sojourns in China. Some twenty-five years later, he returns to Edinburgh and eventually marries a cousin, but finds it difficult to settle: 'I have been a wanderer', he concludes, 'and a child of chance, all my life'.[50]

For some, transportation is an interlude, an interruption or a detour, where unexpected things happen (Patty is speared,

Nicol falls in love)—but afterwards, there is always the expectation of a return home. For others, however, transportation delivers the subject to a final destination, the end point of a series of adventures undertaken elsewhere. Jorgen Jorgenson was born in Copenhagen in 1780 and, like Nicol, he went to sea early on, longing to travel. In October 1800, while at the Cape of Good Hope, he joined the *Lady Nelson*, which had been commissioned to explore and survey parts of southern Australia (Bass Strait, Port Phillip, etc). The ship also accompanied Matthew Flinders' *Investigator* on a survey of the east coast, north of Warrane/Sydney Cove. In 1803 the *Lady Nelson* and Captain John Bowen's *Albion* arrived at the new settlement of piyura kitina/Risdon Cove; camping nearby, Bowen named the site Hobart. So Jorgenson, at this time, played out a foundational role in the colonisation of Australia. He later joined a whaler, and spent time in New Zealand and Brazil, returning to Denmark in 1807, only to find that his birthplace was under sustained attack from the British fleet. This was the Second Battle of Copenhagen, which took place in August and early September of that year. Jorgenson joined the battle, but eventually surrendered and was taken to England, where he lived for a while on parole. In early 1809 he took command of a ship bringing supplies to Iceland, a colony of Denmark governed at the time by Frederich Trampe. Arriving unannounced, Jorgenson placed Trampe under arrest, threw off 'the intolerable yoke of ... Danish oppression', and (inspired by the revolutions in America and France) declared himself head of a new republic, all 'without the firing of a shot or the shedding of a drop of human blood'.[51]

In London later on, he was arrested for the coup and sent to prison. Over the next few years, Jorgenson drank and gambled heavily, was involved in various plots and misadventures across Europe, and finally returned to London. Hopelessly in debt, he was sent to Newgate Prison and sentenced to be transported for seven years. Placed on the hulk *Justitia* at Woolwich (he describes the terrible conditions there), he was then taken to the *Woodman*, with around 150 other convicts. They arrived in Van Diemen's Land on 29 April 1826. Looking back at England as the ship departs, he writes: 'I saw myself an exile and a captive on that element on which I had once been a commander'.[52] Jorgenson had been in the colonies twenty-three years earlier at a founding moment of colonisation, but he finally returned as a convict. As the novelist James Francis Hogan expressed it in his 1891 introduction to Jorgenson's memoirs, this was 'a striking instance of a man of considerable natural abilities making shipwreck of his life'.[53]

Hogan's *The Convict King, Being the Life and Adventures of Jorgen Jorgenson* was effectively a reprint of the memoirs Jorgenson had originally published in Ross's *Hobart Town Almanack and Van Diemen's Land Annual* in 1835 (Part I) and 1838 (Part II, which follows James Porter's account of the seizing of the *Frederick*, discussed above). 'Who so able to write a man's life as the living man himself?' Jorgenson's memoir begins, immodestly enough:

> A Homer is no longer wanted to immortalise an Agamemnon. For where is now the man not qualified to sing his own praise—to sound the trumpet of his own

> exploits? No! Having been promised a niche in *Ross's Van Diemen's Land Annual*—the only sanctuary and safe retreat of great names, the sole Westminster Abbey which these Australian regions can yet boast—I hasten to fill it up before a greater man steps in to occupy the ground.[54]

This is the paranoia of colonial adventure: will someone else be the first in the race to 'occupy the ground'? In Hobart Town, Jorgenson is free to work, getting an appointment with the Van Diemen's Land Company. These are the earlier years of the Tasmanian War, and he goes on expeditions inland that are close in kind to 'roving parties', dealing punitively with palawa people, who by 1829 were regarded as being in open warfare with settlers. 'I was altogether two years in quest of the blacks', Jorgenson writes. In fact, he is made a constable in the Oatlands district, north of nipaluna/Hobart, trying to regulate a settler economy that itself seems almost entirely criminalised.[55] Here, he meets Norah Corbett, one of sixty female convicts and their children who arrived in Van Diemen's Land on the *Persian* in August 1827. Corbett had been arrested as part of a gang of sheep stealers and had turned witness against them. Jorgenson took her into his protection (at great risk to them both) and they embarked on a volatile affair, eventually marrying in early 1831. This would seem to be Jorgenson's first dedicated romance, and it is transportation that brings these two people together. For Hogan, Jorgenson's earlier adventures were examples of 'itinerant vagabondage'.[56] But in Van Diemen's Land, Jorgenson is drawn into the brutally racist business of colonisation, a settler and an agent of the law. The marriage, however, was difficult to sustain. Jorgenson and his wife were often arrested for drunken disorderliness; Norah would also be charged with assault. She died aged thirty-five on 17 July 1840, with Jorgenson reflecting on her 'melancholy state'.[57] Jorgenson himself died six months later.

~

The first convict novel published in the colonies—by the Hobart Town printer, Henry Melville—was Henry Savery's *Quintus Servinton* (1830). Savery was born in 1791 in Bristol, a city that was heavily involved in the sugar industry, taking its product from slave plantations in the Caribbean. He part owned a sugar-refining house on Nelson Street; in 1819 (twelve years after the slave trade itself was abolished in Britain) the building burned down, an event that made its way into his quasi-autobiographical novel, where the business is uninsured and the protagonist, Servinton, loses a significant amount of money. Savery was later convicted of forging bills and was transported to Van Diemen's Land on the *Medway*, arriving in the colony on 14 December 1825. His wife, Eliza, arrived with their son just over two years later, when Savery was about to be imprisoned for debt. He attempted suicide but recovered; Eliza and her son left the colony and returned to England without him a few months later.

We should note that *Quintus Servinton* is not an adventure narrative. As the renowned Tasmanian bibliographer and psychologist E Morris Miller once remarked, Savery 'failed to let himself go in full blast'.[58] Events move at a snail's pace—there are soirées and walks in the countryside; a coach journey to London ('they proceeded at a slow rate') is about as adventurous as the first two volumes of this triple decker actually get.[59] Servinton marries Emily Clifton and they have a son. He is ambitious but short-tempered and self-centred; the novel doesn't like its protagonist much. He never thinks about Caribbean sugar plantations and has nothing to say about slavery. Later on, when his situation is financially precarious, Servinton gets involved with a swindler, Mr Glossover. He writes fraudulent bills and is eventually (well into the third volume) transported to the colonies, a voyage that is almost free of incident, except for the sighting of a remote 'outward bound Indiaman' (a large merchant ship licensed to an East India Company).

When he arrives in Van Diemen's Land, Servinton is employed in a government office and continues to do the kind of accounting work he did in Bristol, oblivious to events around him. These are again the early years of the Tasmanian War, when people like Jorgen Jorgenson were involved in punitive roving parties on the island. But Servinton never notices palawa people, and never encounters or remarks on any kind of frontier violence or lawlessness. It is as if the colony is a sequestered bureaucratic cocoon. The prisons themselves are relatively benign and he is well treated. Emily and her son join him in Van Diemen's Land; a gentleman, Alverney Malvers, sails with her as her 'protector' and seems to want to seduce her later on, trashing Servinton's reputation. Like Eliza, Emily returns to England when her husband's debts land him in prison, and like Savery, Servinton attempts suicide. But the final scenes turn this myopic novel into a melancholy act of wishful thinking. Servinton recovers and is given an 'absolute' pardon, and Emily dutifully returns to Van Diemen's Land to be with him. Reunited, they sail back to England and find 'a quiet, retired spot for our residence', where they live happily.[60] This is another narrative where transportation to the colonies works as a kind of temporary interruption to English life, with characters patiently waiting for it all to be over so they can go back home. In reality, Savery never saw Eliza and his son again. He died at Port Arthur in February 1842, sent there by the colony's magistrate and attorney-general, Algernon Montagu (the real version of the novel's Alverney Malvers), who was appointed as 'protector' to Savery's wife when she had sailed back out to the colony earlier on.

A discussion of the two greatest convict transportation adventures of the nineteenth century will open up some profound contrasts with Savery's slow-moving, relatively benign *Quintus Servinton*—not least, through their representation of transportation as nothing less than a segue into an unrelenting series of events and experiences in the colonies that are almost entirely defined by extreme violence and intense physical and mental suffering. This is colonial adventure at its darkest and most unforgiving, where the protagonist's body is (literally) stripped, punished and torn open, over and over again, no matter where they are sent. James Rosenberg Tucker was transported on the convict ship *Midas* in October 1826, arriving at Warrane/Sydney Cove in February 1827. It is generally accepted that Tucker is the author of a remarkable colonial transportation adventure novel, *Ralph Rashleigh, or The Life of an Exile* (c.1845). This novel did not appear in print until 1929, when Jonathan Cape published a transcript of the found manuscript (as *The Adventures of Ralph Rashleigh*) made by the Sydney librarian Charles Bertie. In 1952 Angus & Robertson published a new, unabridged Australian edition of the novel, edited by Colin Roderick. The novel's protagonist, Ralph Rashleigh, grows up in London, a 'cunning and resourceful ... petty malefactor'.[61] Turning increasingly to crime, he is arrested after a bank robbery and sent to Newgate, where he is stripped, attacked by other prisoners, and later sentenced to hang. At the last minute, the sentence is commuted to transportation and he is placed on a hulk, the *Leviathan*. He escapes, is recaptured and sent back to the hulk, and severely flogged. 'The first dozen strokes from the knotted raw-hide lash were like jagged wire tearing furrows in his flesh, and the second dozen seemed like the filling of the furrows with molten lead, burning like fire into the molten flesh ... [the salt applied to the wounds afterwards] gave a never-fading memory of the torture of being flayed alive'.[62] At this point, Rashleigh hasn't even left England.

When he recovers, Rashleigh is placed on the *Magnet*, a (fictional) convict ship, under Captain James Boltrope. As it sails from Portsmouth to New South Wales, the ship itself becomes a site of violence, with thefts, a mutiny, killings and more floggings. In Warrane/Sydney, it seems for a moment as if Rashleigh—assigned to work for a schoolmaster—might live a peaceful colonial life. But he is soon arrested and sent to work at Emu Plains, where he is subjected to the first of many brutal experiences: flogged, lacerated, chained in irons and made witness to a litany of horrors. Each time Rashleigh escapes his predicament, he is faced with something worse. A sympathetic constable takes him away from a cruel master but locks him up with some bushrangers, who later burn the constable and his family alive in their home. The bushrangers force Rashleigh to join their gang as they wreak havoc in the colony; it is not long before he is 'almost insane with disgust at the wretchedness of the life he was compelled to lead'.[63]

Arrested and threatened again with execution, he is transported to Mulubinba/Newcastle for three years' hard labour. Around 130 convicts are stripped naked and chained close together in the hull of a small convict ship, prompting Rashleigh to think about 'the conditions obtaining in the slave trade'.[64] The military commandment—a man of 'ruthless severity'—gives us a sense of the actual historical moment of the novel. He is most likely based on Lieutenant Colonel James Morisset, who was the penal colony's commandant from 1818 to the end of 1823, when the site was finally declared a free settlement. Christine Wright has noted that 'the largest number of lashes ordered by Morisset was 100 lashes for absconding into the bush'.[65] In the novel, 'Give him a hundred!' is the commandment's refrain of choice. The penal settlement is 'an orgy of punishment ... hour after hour', with the coal mines and lime pits the convicts work in—stripped naked again—reminding Rashleigh of an 'inferno'.[66]

It is often noted that *Ralph Rashleigh* is a narrative in the eighteenth-century British picaresque tradition of Daniel Defoe or Tobias Smollett.[67] But picaresque novels like Defoe's *Roxana: The Fortunate Mistress* (1724) or Smollett's *The Adventures of Peregrine Pickle* (1751) are nowhere near as mercilessly violent and punishing, dark as they can sometimes be.

A more obvious precursor here is the Marquis de Sade and what we can call the 'Sadean picaresque'. De Sade's *Justine, or The Misfortunes of Virtue* was written while he was imprisoned in the Bastille in 1787 and published in 1791, quickly becoming a best-seller. Tucker is unlikely to have known *Justine*, which wasn't translated into English until 1953.[68] But de Sade's narrative of a fundamentally good character systematically degraded, falsely accused, stripped, ravished, kidnapped and abused by bandits, thrown into prisons, threatened with execution, and flogged often to the point of death by one tyrant after another, seems strikingly close in kind to the convict experiences of Ralph Rashleigh in the colonies.

In her commentary on de Sade's novel, Frances Ferguson notes Justine's sustaining delusion, that each time she escapes her captors 'there might be a genuinely sympathetic individual over the horizon'.[69] In Tucker's novel, Rashleigh has no such delusion; but there is one event that does eventually offer him a prolonged moment of respite from his ongoing torment. With some convicts, he finally escapes from Mulubinba/Newcastle in a boat. There is a chase and a battle with Aboriginal people, with deaths on both sides. At a river mouth, a sudden flood and a blast of thunder cause Rashleigh to lose consciousness. When he awakes, he is surrounded by Aboriginal people, including an elder with 'terrible scars', 'one of those strange creatures, called *carandjies*'.[70] The novel means *koradji*, a Dharug word (although Rashleigh is much further north) for someone with traditional skills in medicine, a 'clever man'. He is taken to their camp and initiated, the scars on his body blending with the wounds of the lash. He is given a wife, Lorra, the koradji becomes his foster father, and he remains with this community as a cohabitant for four years; a calm—'steady and uneventful'—interlude in the midst of his otherwise harrowing adventures.[71] This is a remarkable moment in a colonial novel, where a white character learns to become 'Aboriginal', his life—and his appearance (his skin is dyed black)—utterly transformed to the point of being unrecognisable to other colonials. But when the koradji dies, Rashleigh loses his status and struggles to protect his wife, who is killed by some rival men. Overcome by grief, he goes on a rampage of revenge, mourning Lorra's death, 'the only woman, outside his family, who had ever loved him'.[72] Leaving the community at last, he travels along the coast with two Aboriginal women, Tita and Enee. Meeting many different Aboriginal communities along the way, he is 'always received hospitably and allowed to remain as long as he wished in their camps, and to depart when he pleased'.[73]

The colonial castaway adventure involving prolonged cohabitation with Aboriginal people will be the topic of Chapter 3. Here, in *Ralph Rashleigh*, it works to take the protagonist away from a colonial experience exclusively defined by punishment and laceration, and it gives him freedom of movement across country that he would not otherwise have had. With his companions, Rashleigh makes his way to the northeastern tip of Cape York, where they find a shipwreck with two women and a child still on board. The women believe he is a 'New Holland aborigine' and he maintains the illusion, building a rough dwelling in a cave, where they all live for a while as a kind of extended castaway family. A trading ship comes looking for the white women and is soon under attack from (possibly) local Yadhaigana people. Rashleigh makes an important but fateful decision: he decides to fight with the captain and his crew, confessing to one of the women, Mrs Marby, that 'the man who had seemed to her a hero was really a convict masquerading as an aborigine'.[74] Back in Warrane/Sydney, he literally becomes white again, cleansing his skin. The two Aboriginal women distance themselves from him as he takes a job as an overseer on a farming property, working hard and gaining a reputation 'as a man of scrupulous integrity'.[75] Rashleigh hears that squatters at a place that used to be called Beardy Plains (now Glen Innes), north of Mulubinba/Newcastle, are struggling with Ngoorabul people over their country. He goes to help the squatters but is speared and killed, his body 'terribly butchered'.[76]

The ending of the novel gives this convict a violent death just as he is about to become a settler in the service of the colony, working to kill and dispossess Aboriginal people—despite the fact that he had earlier lived with an Aboriginal community for four years. We might think about the ending of de Sade's *Justine* by way of comparison here: Justine is struck and killed by a lightning bolt just as she is about to be welcomed back into society. In *Ralph Rashleigh*, a young convict finally escapes the torment of penal institutions and —forgetting the earlier interlude of his 'Aboriginal' life—is welcomed back into the colony. But this means he must willingly participate in the violent business of colonisation and frontier expansion, and it seems as if the novel decides that this is why he cannot be allowed to live.

Marcus Clarke's *His Natural Life* was originally published in serial form in the *Australian Journal* between March

1870 and June 1872 (Clarke was its editor for some of this time). It was then revised and published as a novel by George Robertson in Melbourne in 1874; by Richard Bentley in London (in three, heavily edited, volumes) in 1875; and by Harpers in the United States in 1876. A reviewer in *Harper's Magazine* complained that Clarke's account of the British convict transportation system made it rival 'in atrocity the terrible processes of the Inquisition'.[77] Later editions, beginning with Richard Bentley's reprint in 1882, used the title *For the Term of His Natural Life*. By this time, of course, convict transportation to the colonies had come to an end. So this is a historical novel; in fact, it begins in May 1827, around the time James Tucker had arrived as a convict in New South Wales.

In England, Sir Richard Devine is a shipbuilder and naval contractor. He tells his wife, Lady Ellinor Wade, that he knows her lover, Lord Bellasis, is the true father of their wayward son, Richard Devine. Disinheriting Devine, he instead promises his fortune to his sister's son, Maurice Frere, whose family (rather like Henry Savery and Quintus Servinton) had seen the abolition of the slave trade ruin their Bristol business. Later that evening, Richard Devine stumbles across the murdered body of Lord Bellasis, and is arrested and tried for the crime. To protect his mother, he immediately changes his name to Rufus Dawes. Found not guilty of murder but guilty of robbing the corpse, he is then sentenced to transportation to the colonies on the convict ship *Malabar* (which had in fact last carried convicts to Van Diemen's Land in 1821). Aboard is Captain John Vickers, soon to be the new commandant of the Macquarie Harbour penal settlement in Van Diemen's Land.

He is accompanied by his wife, Julia, and their six-year-old daughter, Sylvia. Maurice Frere is also on board and is romantically attracted to Julia's maid, Sarah Purfoy. Other convicts in the novel are also introduced, including the giant, Gabbett—who, like Dickens's Magwitch, had returned to England before his sentence had expired, only to be transported again—and the forger John Rex. Rex also turns out to be a son of Lord Bellasis, and Sarah Purfoy is his wife.

The penal settlement itself resembles an underworld, with the convict ship sailing into Parralaongatek/Macquarie Harbour through its opening, Hell's Gates, a 'pit of torment' that contains 'the most dreaded of all the houses of bondage'.[78] The novel shifts to December 1833, with Rufus Dawes—shunned, abused, and driven to 'personal abasement and self-loathing'[79]—sent to solitary confinement on Grummet Island, after a failed attempt at absconding with Gabbett and some other convicts. This is the beginning of the evacuation of this particular penal colony, and Clarke in fact draws on James Porter's memoir—discussed above—to recreate these events. We recall that in January 1834, as Macquarie Harbour was being cleared, Porter and nine other convicts commandeered the *Frederick* and set sail for South America. Clarke had already written about Porter's memoir in his collection of historical essays, *Old Tales of a Young Country* (1871). In *His Natural Life*, the *Frederick* becomes the *Osprey*. Clarke lists the names of the convicts who had in fact seized the ship, including Porter, and then adds John Rex to the list as their leader. 'I'll take her round the world', he tells his crew, ventriloquising the actual convict John Barker as they sail off, leaving

Frere behind with Julia Vickers and her daughter Sylvia, who waves the mutineers goodbye. Clarke follows Porter's memoir by taking the mutineers across the Pacific to Valdivia, and then to China, where they are caught and sent back to Van Diemen's Land. Porter's memoir was published locally, in Hobart. But Clarke gives the convict mutineers much greater prominence as global adventurers, their story soon 'dramatised at a London theatre' with a 'popular novelist ... engaged in a work descriptive of their wondrous fortune'.[80] Sylvia later reads about them, her imagination stirred by 'the leaky brig, the South American slavery, the midnight escape'.[81]

At the now-abandoned Macquarie Harbour site, Rufus Dawes joins the marooned Frere, along with Julia and her 'golden' daughter—who reduces the convict to tears in one of many heavily sentimentalised encounters between these two characters. Living for a while with Sylvia and the others at this apparently empty place on the west coast of Van Diemen's Land, this is Dawes's castaway moment. Like Defoe's Crusoe, he catches goats and skins them, and even builds a boat, becoming 'an active member of ... a society of four'.[82] This is his calm interlude, a brief period of respite from his torments, where he almost forgets he is a convict. It is worth comparing these scenes with Ralph Rashleigh's peaceful few years with an Aboriginal community on Australia's north-east coast. In Van Diemen's Land around this time, the government agent, George Augustus Robinson, had been forcibly removing palawa people to islands off the western coast, as a colonial solution to the ongoing Tasmanian War. Robinson had in fact visited Parralaongatek/Macquarie Harbour in April 1830 and again in

1833, detaining palawa people on islands (including Grummet Island) at the penal settlement, where many died. (These are early instances of a process of island incarceration that continues in Australia today.) All surviving palawa people were taken from Parralaongatek /Macquarie Harbour to Wybalenna on Flinders Island in November 1833, just a couple of months before the penal settlement was cleared and Dawes and the others were marooned there. But there is no mention of palawa people in Clarke's novel, no record of the Tasmanian War or any kind of Aboriginal dispossession in Van Diemen's Land, and no account of palawa people at the Macquarie Harbour site itself. In contrast to *Ralph Rashleigh*, *His Natural Life* completely erases Aboriginal people from its narrative.

In Hobart Town five years later, Sylvia is engaged to Maurice Frere (she thinks he saved her life) and has some kind of amnesia about Dawes, who has been sent to Premaydena/ Port Arthur. John Rex tries to convince Dawes to abscond with some of the convicts, including Gabbett. With Sarah Purfoy's help, Rex himself manages to get to a ship and he returns to England, impersonating Dawes/Richard Devine in a failed attempt to claim the family inheritance (he later confesses to the murder of Lord Bellasis). In the meantime, the novel follows Gabbett and a small group of convicts as they make their way across south-eastern Van Diemen's Land. This is the opposite of Rex's earlier escape on the *Osprey* with James Porter, which led to a journey that, in Clarke's novel, at least, makes them famous as global adventurers. Gabbett's escape is local and strictly limited in range; and it turns out to be very dark, with Gabbett finally caught, the only survivor, 'a gaunt and blood-stained man' with human flesh in his bag.[83] This gruesome figure is based on the notorious 'cannibal' convict Alexander Pearce, although Pearce himself had in fact been caught and hanged in 1824 after escaping from Parralaongatek/Macquarie Harbour.

The novel then shifts to 1846, with Dawes now a convict on Norfolk Island. By this time—historically speaking—the commandant and prison reformer Alexander Maconochie had left the island, replaced by much harsher administrators: Joseph Childs from February 1844, and then, in August 1846, John Price. Price came from a family of slave owners, with sugar plantations in Jamaica. He arrived in Hobart Town in May 1836 and went on to become a notoriously severe police magistrate. At Norfolk Island, he began his tenure 'by hanging a dozen mutineers' and was soon accused by the prison chaplain, the Rev. Thomas Rogers, 'of "ferocious severity"', including the punishment of 'chaining men to a wall in spread-eagle position with an iron bit in the mouth'.[84] In Clarke's novel, the Rev. Mr North is based on Thomas Rogers, while Maurice Frere—who comes to Norfolk Island as its new commandant while Dawes is there, and whose family had made (and lost) their fortune from slavery and sugar plantations—is based on Price.

His Natural Life takes Rufus Dawes from Parralaongatek/Macquarie Harbour to Premaydena/Port Arthur and finally to Norfolk Island, conveying a sense of the colonies as little more than a network of penal institutions to which one is perpetually condemned. Even the absconders—Rex, Porter and the others on the *Osprey*, Gabbett—either die or are eventually caught and brought back. The novel isn't picaresque like *Ralph Rashleigh*, because its protagonist isn't allowed to be itinerant and move from one event to another, completely different event. Instead, his trajectory is relentlessly determined for him, and every destination is the same as the one before—or perhaps slightly worse. But it is indeed Sadean, with punishment and degradation as its primary drivers. When Frere arrives at Norfolk Island, 'The cords of discipline are suddenly drawn tight', and the convicts are flogged over and over, 'reduced to a continual agony of terror and self-loathing'.[85] Frere focuses his Sadean rage on Dawes in particular, relishing the sight of 'the lacerated body'.[86] He sets about torturing Dawes, strapping him to an iron 'stretcher' that requires him to hold his unsupported head up or suffocate. Sylvia, now Frere's wife, arrives on the island and demands that Dawes is cut down. In a final flurry of scenes, the Rev. Mr North confesses his love for Sylvia and tells Dawes he witnessed the murder of his father, Lord Bellasis, in England long ago, also admitting that he was the one who robbed the corpse.

Rather than the Sadean picaresque, Clarke's novel is a Sadean melodrama, full of hidden secrets, exclamatory confessions and remarkable coincidences. Dawes puts on North's cloak and escapes into the night, getting on board a schooner that also carries Sylvia. A storm approaches and as lightning strikes, 'Rufus Dawes comprehends that the elements had come to destroy him'—not unlike the end of Sade's *Justine*.[87] In an epilogue, the wreck of the schooner is discovered, with Sylvia and Dawes both dead and in each other's arms. We have seen the prison reformer's view that transportation should not be worse than death. But as one reviewer put it in 1874, Clarke's novel tells us 'that transportation may be [even] more terrible'.[88]

CHAPTER 3

Castaways and Cohabitations

In *Ralph Rashleigh*, as we have seen, the convict protagonist escapes his incarceration at one point and spends four years cohabiting with an Aboriginal community somewhere along the northern coast of Queensland. This is a rare moment in colonial fiction, but in fact examples of cohabitation with Aboriginal communities in the colonies themselves were not especially uncommon. This chapter will look at the experiences of convicts and others who, whether by choice or by accident, took time out from the colony to live with the people colonisation aimed to subdue, dispossess, demonise and kill. It will also look at the way those experiences have been represented. The sources here are the written accounts, which can take various narrative forms: first-hand recollections, official records, media commentaries, testimonies and so on. Angela Woollacott has described first- and second-hand accounts of several non-Aboriginal women who had cohabited with Aboriginal people as '[s]tories of colonial misadventure'.[1] This seems like a useful way of thinking about such encounters, generally speaking: as 'misadventures' that saw people in or on their way to the colony literally go off course or simply walk away and leave, in some cases for a remarkably long period of time. The nature and length of these encounters could significantly transform those people, changing their perspective on the colony—and on colonisation itself. There are risks and challenges on both sides; the first encounters at the frontier could, of course, be hostile and fatal. But cohabiting with an Aboriginal community prolongs that encounter and, as it gets underway, it can generate new insights, new knowledges, and new ways of living from day to day. At the same time, the expansive pressures of colonisation mean that such encounters are always fragile, limited in scope, and liable to sudden interruption at any time. In this sense, we could see the (mis)adventure of cohabitation as a unique experience of what Penelope Edmonds and Amanda Nettelbeck have called 'precarious intimacy'.[2]

David Collins was the judge advocate and secretary of New South Wales in the 1790s, and his record of these early years, *An Account of the English Colony in New South Wales* (1798), is one of the foundational texts of Australia's colonisation. In an entry for February 1795, Collins writes about James Wilson, an ex-convict, who informs him that Dharug people along Dyarubbin/the Hawkesbury River are seeking retribution after mistreatment by some local settlers. Collins seems both intrigued and disturbed by this man, who had been living for some time with a Dharug community:

> Wilson, a wild idle young man ... preferred living among natives in the vicinity of the river, to earning the wages of honest industry by working for settlers. He had formed

> an intermediate language between his own and theirs, with which he made shift to comprehend something of what they wished him to communicate; for they did not conceal the sense they entertained of the injuries which had been done to them. The tribe with whom Wilson associated had given him a name, Bun-bo-é ... As the gratifying [of] an idle disposition was the sole object with Wilson in herding with these people, no good consequence was likely to ensue from it; and it was by no means improbable, that at some future time, if disgusted with the white people, he would join the blacks, and assist them in committing depredations, or make use of their assistance to punish or revenge his own injuries.[3]

This is a colonial administrator's view of someone who (for him) has inexplicably left the settlement to live with Aboriginal people. Collins thinks Wilson must be 'idle', because he simply refuses to contribute to the 'honest industry' of the colony. But Wilson is also transgressive, crossing a boundary and radically shifting his perspective on colonisation as a consequence. In Collins's account, Wilson is like a *maron*, a term discussed in Chapter 1 that was once applied both to escaped cattle and runaway slaves: 'herding with these people'. The very idea leads to a curious kind of colonial paranoia: what if Wilson becomes so 'disgusted' with the colony that he actively turns against it? On the other hand, Collins sees value in Wilson as an intermediary, someone who can communicate back and forth between settlers and the Dharug people. His liminality, potentially at least, is useful. As Grace Karskens puts it in

People of the River (2020), her study of early settler contact along Dyarubbin/the Hawkesbury River, 'In demonstrating that it was possible to live in the bush with Aboriginal people ... [Wilson] effectively struck at the whole colonial project ... At the same time, Bunboé's experience, knowledge and skills also meant that he was extremely valuable to the authorities, so they made use of him'.[4]

Karskens comments, too, on Bunboé, Wilson's Dharug name. Wilson had supposedly told a Dharug woman that he was her son, returned from the dead. But Karskens suggests the local community 'were well aware of his deception, for *buna* was a word meaning "to speak falsely, in jest, or to make believe," while *boé* or *bò-ye* was the word for dead'.[5] Wilson/Bunboé had been scarified, but Karskens suggests that he was 'never fully accepted' by his adopted community.[6] Even so, he was soon joined by a convict, William Knight, who 'thinking there must be some sweets in the life which Wilson led, determined to share them with him, and went off to the woods'.[7] In August 1795 Collins reported that two men came into the settlement apparently 'for the purpose of forcing a wife from among the women of the district' and 'were discovered, each dragging a girl by the arm (whose age could not have been beyond nine or ten years) assisted by their new associates'.[8] Wilson and Knight were caught and imprisoned, but soon escaped to live once more with the Dharug.

Victoria K Haskins and Worimi historian John Maynard have commented on this event, speculating that perhaps the Dharug had asked the white men to 'pick out young wives for themselves from among their own race'; they even wonder if it was an act of retaliation, 'a forthright declaration of revenge for the taking of Aboriginal girls by white settlers'.[9] In early 1796 Collins does indeed note that Wilson and Knight seem to have joined with Dharug people in their reprisals against settlers. He makes a fascinating observation: 'They demonstrated to the natives of how little use a musquet was when once discharged, and this effectively removed that terror of our fire-arms with which it had been our constant endeavour to inspire them'.[10] This is a remarkable moment, which sees two ordinary white men completely demystify colonial power ('terror') for the Aboriginal people who are fighting against it. Two years later, Wilson was appointed by Governor John Hunter as a guide in an expedition party across Gulu-Mada/the Blue Mountains: so he was willing to serve the colony's interests as well. He returned to the Dharug people again soon afterwards and seems to have attempted to take an Aboriginal woman as his wife. 'Clansman or not', Karskens remarks, 'he was speared to death'.[11]

Wilson's liminality is a defining feature of cohabitation as a particular kind of colonial misadventure. He benefits from living both in the colony and with Aboriginal people, apparently moving freely back and forth between the two; and yet he also doesn't quite belong with either. For Karskens, Wilson could never be fully integrated by Dharug people. But was it possible for a white colonial *ever* to be fully accepted into an Aboriginal community? Perhaps the closest we come to an example of this is William Buckley. Born in Cheshire in 1780, Buckley later left an apprenticeship as a bricklayer to serve with the English navy, fighting against Napoleon in the Netherlands. Later, in England, he was convicted of receiving some stolen cloth and sentenced to fourteen years' transportation. Placed on the convict ship *Calcutta*, Buckley arrived at Nerm/Port Phillip Bay in October 1803. With two other convicts, he soon absconded from the fledgling colony, 'dissatisfied with my condition as a prisoner of the Crown'.[12] Separating from his companions, he headed north, hoping 'to reach Sydney which I believed was not far off'.[13] Not long afterwards, he reports, 'I fell in with an Old Black fishing near the sea with his wife and a large family of children' and 'was treated with the greatest kindness, partook of their food and laboured with them'.[14] This delightfully casual encounter ('I fell in with ...')—and the experience of Aboriginal hospitality and shared labour—in fact marked the beginning of an ongoing cohabitation with Wadawurrung people in the region that lasted more than thirty years, until 6 July 1835.

There are two colonial records of Buckley's experiences, both presented as transcriptions of his first-hand oral testimony. The earlier one (from which the quotations above are taken) is a short narrative 'dictated' to the Port Phillip Bay missionary George Langhorne in 1837—although it wasn't published until 1891, when a relative of Langhorne's gave the manuscript to the Melbourne *Argus*.[15] The title of the manuscript itself—now held at the State Library of Victoria—is *Reminiscences of James Buckley who lived for Thirty Years among the Wallawarro or Watourong Tribes at Geelong Port Phillip communicated by him to George Langhorne*. (Langhorne was mistaken about Buckley's first name.) But the *Argus* published it under the heading 'Buckley, the Wild White Man: An Original Narrative'. The 'wild white man' was a description that had been circulating since the 1850s; it at least captures the transgression involved here, of someone who had willingly crossed over the frontier to live with Aboriginal people for such a long period of time. Arriving at a Wadawurrung community, women weep to see him: 'I learnt afterwards', Buckley says, 'that they believed me to be a black who had died some time since and who had come again to them in the shape of a white man'.[16]

In this early account, Buckley is cast in quite a different way from Wilson: much more willing to recognise and adapt to the protocols of the people he now resides with. 'I lived as they lived', he says, 'and was careful not to give them offence in the smallest thing—yielding to them at all times'.[17] He comes to learn the Wadawurrung people's language and, after several years in the community, begins to forget how to speak English. He also learns to hunt and fish like an 'expert'. Langhorne's manuscript conveys a sense that Buckley's relationship with the Wadawurrung (spelt 'Watourongs' here) was not about hostility or mistrust, but about mutual respect, trust and care. As he becomes more aware of increasing numbers of settlers arriving to occupy the site of what would become Naarm/Melbourne, Buckley wonders if he could ever return to the colony: 'I never supposed I should be comfortable among my own countrymen again'.[18] In a later reprint of this manuscript, in the *Age* in July 1911, Langhorne is quoted as remarking of Buckley, not long after he had finally returned to the colony, 'He appeared to me always discontented and dissatisfied, and I believe it would have been a great relief to him had the settlement been abandoned, and he [was] left alone with his sable friends'.[19] In this account, such a prolonged cohabitation with the Wadawurrung leaves Buckley with no enthusiasm at all for the business of colonisation.

But the second colonial record of Buckley's life with the Wadawurrung is very different. John Morgan's *The Life and Adventures of William Buckley* was published in Hobart in 1852, just a few years before Buckley's death. A journalist and liberal reformer, Morgan was a strong advocate for colonial development. He interviewed Buckley in the years after his return to the colony, and the narrative itself is in Buckley's voice. But it is generally agreed that Morgan both wrote and significantly transformed this account of Buckley's experiences.[20] 'I cherish the hope of my adventures being read elsewhere, as well as in the Australian Colonies', Buckley says at one point, ventriloquising Morgan's wishful thinking as a local author. Morgan casts Buckley's early escape from the fledgling colony as Robinsonade castaway narrative, with Buckley initially finding shelter in a cave by the ocean, 'my Robinson Crusoe hut upon the surface of the waters'.[21] The first encounter with Wadawurrung people here is quite different from that first relaxed, hospitable encounter in Langhorne's *Reminiscences*: 'I thought I heard the sound of human voices; and, on looking up, was somewhat startled at seeing three natives standing on the high land immediately above me. They were armed with spears, and had opossum skins thrown over their shoulders, partially covering their bodies. Standing as they did, on an elevated position, armed too, and being myself totally defenceless, I confess I felt alarmed'.[22] Left alone at the camp, Buckley decides to leave but almost immediately regrets it. Later on, he takes a spear from a burial mound, using it as a walking stick. Asleep beside a tree, he is seen by some Wadawurrung people, who take him to their community, feed him, and give him a name, Murrangurk, 'which I afterwards learnt was the name of a man formerly belonging to their tribe, who had been buried at the spot where I had found the piece of spear I still carried with me'.[23] The spear places Buckley into a family network, and soon he finds himself 'tolerably at home' in the community.[24]

It is interesting to consider the question of how 'at home' Buckley may have been with Aboriginal people during this time. In the 1890s the Kwatkwat artist Tommy McRae [Yackaduna or Warra-euea] produced a number of ink drawings of Buckley with Wadawurrung men, one of which (*Corroboree*) shows him participating in a ceremonial dance in traditional dress and body paint but wearing a settler's hat: almost, but perhaps not quite, fully integrated into the community. There are varying views on whether Buckley was in any kind of sustained relationship with Aboriginal women. Morgan suggests he was given a wife and adopted some children, and later cohabited with 'a female friend' who had left her community 'at some distance'.[25] In his 1881 study of Aboriginal languages and life in the western districts of Victoria, the colonial ethnographer James Dawson provided another perspective on this relationship. He drew on an account given by a Buninyong woman, Purranmurnin Tallarwurnin, to William Goodall, director during this time of the Framlingham Aboriginal Station, a mission that had operated in Girai Wurrung Country from the 1850s to 1890. Described as 'the wife of the white man Buckley at the time he was found by the first settlers in Victoria', her recollection offers a different version of the first encounter with Buckley, with Wadawurrung people 'very much alarmed' by the sight of him asleep on the ground—in contrast to Buckley's own alarm in Morgan's narrative.[26] 'At length',

Goodall reports, 'one of the party finding courage addressed him as muurnong guurk (meaning that they supposed him to be one who had been killed and come to life again) ....'[27] They 'soon became friends' and eventually Buckley is 'recognised as one of the tribe'.[28] In Morgan's account, he later reflects on his three decades with the Wadawurrung people 'with inexpressible astonishment; considering it, as it were, altogether a dreaming delusion, and not reality'.[29] This may be Morgan ventriloquising Buckley's own thoughts; interestingly, it casts the cohabitation adventure as a kind of Rip Van Winkle interlude, where the very idea of colonisation drops out of a white colonial man's consciousness for an extended period of time.

Morgan's *Life and Adventures* is more overtly racist than Langhorne's earlier *Reminiscences*, talking up various acts of Aboriginal 'savagery' and 'treachery' with the aim (familiar enough in colonial adventure narratives) of shocking or appalling readers both locally and abroad. Published fifteen years after Langhorne, Morgan also chronicled the aftermath of Buckley's return to the colony in July 1835, which marked the end of his cohabitation adventure (his 'dreaming delusion'). By this time, John Batman had arrived from Van Diemen's Land to play a leading role in the colonisation of Port Phillip, the establishment of Melbourne, and the mass dispossession of Aboriginal people from the region. Buckley was soon drafted into the service of the colony, assisting Batman and surveyor John Wedge in their dealings with local elders.

In Langhorne's earlier narrative, Buckley would have been pleased to see settlement 'abandoned'. Morgan's account sees him eventually participating in the business of colonisation, but he is at least allowed to retain some critical distance: 'I looked upon the land dealing spoken of, as another hoax of the white man'.[30] Like James Wilson, he became an intermediary figure, an interpreter and negotiator, attempting where he could to make the rapid expansion of colonial settlement less violent, less traumatic, for both Aboriginal people and settlers—but mostly for the latter. Gaining a free pardon, he is grateful for 'the confidence thus placed in my future exertions to benefit the first settlers'.[31] The free pardon may well have been the colony's way of securing his services and, certainly, he never absconded again. In England, Buckley had worked as a bricklayer. In the colony, he helped to build John Batman's house: 'I superintended the putting up of the chimneys'.[32]

Perhaps the most famous, or infamous, example of colonial cohabitation took place just one year after Buckley returned to the colony in the winter of 1835—having spent more than thirty years with Wadawurrung people—and it was almost fleeting by comparison. Surviving a shipwreck and eventually making it to shore in an open boat, Eliza Fraser lived for around seven weeks—from June to August 1836—with Butchulla (or Badtjala) people on K'gari, a large island north of Queensland's Sunshine Coast.[33] For Kay Schaffer, the story of Fraser's cohabitation became 'a foundational fiction for Australia', because she was the first white woman to live with Aboriginal people and then document her story.[34] Her *Narrative of the Capture, Sufferings, and Miraculous Escape of Mrs Eliza Fraser* was published in New

York in 1837. This was the first of many versions of Fraser's experiences on the island, its title—turning cohabitation into 'capture'—immediately identifying the narrative as sensational and melodramatic (one reason why it became a foundational *fiction*). It was in fact discussed as a 'colonial captivity narrative' —a genre about imperilled white women in the colonies in need of rescuing from Aboriginal people, invariably by men—in some insightful feminist cultural criticism from the 1990s.[35] More recently, in her excellent book *Finding Eliza: Power and Colonial Storytelling* (2016), the Eualeyai/Gamillaroi academic Larissa Behrendt regards such lurid captivity narratives as necessary elements in the ongoing demonisation of Aboriginal people by colonial settlers—a demonisation that helped to rationalise dispossession: 'These stories became an important part of the colonising process,' she writes, 'because they illustrated the reasons given to justify the taking of Aboriginal land. They became part of the popular narrative of Australian history—the white man battling the elements and taming the wild land and the wild people upon it—for many years.'[36]

The origins of the colonial captivity narrative are generally traced back to North America in the late seventeenth century, with the publication of the remarkably popular *A Narrative of the Captivity and Restoration of Mrs. Mary Rowlandson* (1682). Rowlandson was a Puritan. Her account of her capture by the Wampanoag in Massachusetts is full of violence and horror, a Manichean narrative that refuses the possibility of any cross-cultural understanding between Rowlandson and local Indigenous people. In his book on American captivity narratives, Christopher Castiglia suggests the genre 'offered

American women a female picaresque, an adventure story set, unlike most American women's literature, outside the home'.[37] Like Fraser on K'gari, Rowlandson experiences a relatively brief cohabitation adventure, or misadventure; taken from her home when it is raided, she is finally reunited with her husband after living with the Wampanoag for about eleven weeks. Interestingly, Eliza Fraser's *Narrative of the Capture* was not only first published in the United States but also transposed into an American frontier context, using terms such as 'wigwam', 'squaw' and 'papoose' in its descriptions of Butchulla life—one of several ways of signalling its generic debt to Rowlandson's earlier *A Narrative of the Captivity*.

Fraser herself had left her home (and three children) in Scotland to sail with her husband, Captain James Fraser—Samuel in her *Narrative*—delivering cargo on the *Stirling Castle*. Outbound from Warrane/Sydney to Singapore, the ship ran aground on the Swain Reefs, around 200 kilometres north of K'gari. James Fraser had a poor track record as a captain, and was by this time quite ill. His wife, according to other accounts, was heavily pregnant and gave birth at sea to an infant, who died soon afterwards.[38] The crew saved themselves by getting into several boats, but these soon became separated. Making landfall on a K'gari beach, Eliza Fraser, her husband and several crew were claimed, as she puts it, by 'three different parties of different tribes, or clans' and put into 'bondage'.[39] Her Manichean racism is given full vent in this captivity narrative, which also becomes a chronicle of white slavery. The Butchulla people are 'frightful looking savages', she writes, cruel and brutal, and with 'the ferocity of wild beasts', etc.[40]

The word *savage* has a long etymology, going back to the Old French *sauvage* ('wild') and the Latin word *silvaticus* ('of the woods'). As Kate Fullagar notes, by the nineteenth century the term could signify either ferocity and cruelty, or gentleness, trust and nobility.[41] Fraser's account pretty much embraced the former. The women ('squaws') put her to work and seem to torment her—although (showing trust?) they give her an infant to nurse, a task the Wampanoag had also given to Mary Rowlandson. A few weeks later, she sees her husband—too sick to work—speared and stabbed to death. Another crew member, Brown, is burned alive. A Butchella man comes to her aid when an 'old chief' wants Fraser for his lover, but he is killed. And then, just before the chief can 'accomplish his designs', a government-sanctioned search party rescues her, and 'a man of great bodily strength and courage', John Graham, lifts her up and carries her to safety.[42] She is taken to Moreton Bay (Quandamooka Country) and then to Warrane/Sydney, where she spoke about her ordeal to the newspapers.

Some of the testimonies from other rescued crew from the *Stirling Castle* give different accounts of events on or around K'gari at this time. In a hearing in front of the lord mayor of London in January 1838, Robert Darge (who was in the longboat with Eliza Fraser and her husband) spoke of being put to work but tempered Fraser's claims about Butchulla *savagery*. 'I cannot call them a cruel people', he said, noting that he never saw anyone killed. Darge's testimony is included in the English journalist John Curtis's long, moralising chronicle of these events—published in London in 1838—which talks up the ferocity of the Butchulla and insists on their role as 'heartless task-masters' to the castaways.[43] Darge suggests he was traded between communities, telling the others 'they would all be *coocheed* (coloured with red or black ochre), according to the tribe to which they were assigned'.[44] Sent to work with a different community, he meets two absconded convicts known as Tallboy and Tursi, who have already been living with local Aboriginal people on the island and have no plans to return to the colony. So Eliza Fraser and the crew of the *Stirling Castle* were not the first white cohabitants here (a sign of colonisation's encroachment).

But while some kept their experiences deliberately obscure, others—like Fraser herself—sought to broadcast the story of their (mis)adventures to as wide an audience as possible. Harry Youlden was another *Stirling Castle* survivor, who published his own account of cohabitation on K'gari in a New York literary magazine, the *Knickerbocker*. This is also a captivity narrative—the crew 'longed for deliverance'—but Youlden at least recognises Aboriginal hospitality and is willing to learn about local practices. At one point, he joins a fishing expedition: 'there we then were', he writes, 'black and white, all mixed together, naked'.[45] Eliza Fraser barely features in his narrative, except for a few dismissive (and vividly misogynistic) remarks at the beginning that entirely reject her version of those few weeks on K'gari: 'She was a very vixen ... a terrible liar, and the most profane, artful, wicked woman that ever lived; indeed, coming very near to my idea of the Devil'.[46]

The encounters with Tallboy and Tursi are indeed a reminder of just how many whites left the colony to live with Aboriginal people during the early years of colonisation. John Graham, who had (in her account) rescued Eliza Fraser, arrived in Warrane/Sydney in April 1825 as a convict on the *Hooghley*. He escaped Moreton Bay penal settlement in July 1827 and headed north, stumbling into a Quandamooka camp, where a widowed woman claimed him as her husband. Graham lived with this community for six years; as an early biography obscurely puts it, 'some strange impulse' eventually made him return to Moreton Bay, where he surrendered himself to the authorities.[47] Like Buckley, Graham became an intermediary, valued for his language skills and knowledge, and he accompanied Lieutenant Otter on the rescue mission that brought Fraser, Darge, Youlden and other castaways back to the colony. Graham, Tursi, Tallboy: the Eliza Fraser story seems to draw out one white cohabitant after another. James Davis was also transported to New South Wales in 1825 and was later sent to Moreton Bay. Like Graham, he absconded and headed north, to Wide Bay, living with a local Kabi Kabi community, who adopted him and named him Duramboi (or Durrumboi).

The Butchulla historian Olga Miller has drawn on oral testimony from her family to tell a different story of Fraser's rescue that involves Aboriginal women handing her over to Davis/Duramboi, who then took her to a rescue party not far away.[48] David Bracewell (or Bracefell or Bracefield) was transported in 1826; he also absconded, made his way up to K'gari, and lived there with local communities—who named him Wandi. He claimed to have met Fraser and assisted her, although this has been viewed sceptically.[49] Both Davis/Duramboi and Bracewell/Wandi were eventually taken back to the colony in 1842 by colonial explorer and builder Andrew Petrie. It seemed as if these white men, like Buckley, had more or less forgotten about colonisation altogether during their cohabitation. Davis, Petrie reported, 'looked at us as if he had never seen a white man before'; naked and appearing to have no English, he seemed like 'a wild man of the woods'—that is, a *savage*.[50]

In September 1846 the HMS *Rattlesnake* left Portsmouth to embark on a surveying expedition around the northern coast of Australia. On board was the young TH Huxley—just before he made his reputation as a famous biologist—the marine artist Oswald Walters Brierly and the Scottish-born naturalist John MacGillivray. In his *Narrative of the Voyage of H.M.S. Rattlesnake* (1852), MacGillivray reported the following, as the ship made its way around the top of Cape York:

> On Oct. 16th [1849], a startling incident occurred to break the monotony of our stay. In the afternoon some of our people on shore were surprised to see a young white woman come up to claim their protection from a party of natives from whom she had recently made her escape, and who, she thought, would otherwise bring her back ... Her name is Barbara Thomson [*sic*] ...[51]

Barbara Thompson (*née* Crawford) was a Scottish woman who had emigrated as a child to New South Wales in 1837. When she was about sixteen (perhaps younger), she eloped to Moreton Bay with William Thompson, a whaler. In early 1844 they sailed with a small crew in search of whale oil casks, heading eventually to the Torres Strait, where their cutter was wrecked on a reef. Barbara Thompson managed to survive, rescued by Kuarareg people from Muralag/Prince of Wales Island.

Adopted into a local family, she was given a Kuarareg name, Giom. Thompson/Giom lived on Muralag for over four and a half years. Coming onshore, the crew of the HMS *Rattlesnake* initially mistook her for one of the Kuarareg. This is the passage from MacGillivray's journal that later gave Patrick White the title for a novel, *A Fringe of Leaves* (1976), that was otherwise based on the narrative of Eliza Fraser: 'With the exception of a narrow fringe of leaves in front, she wore no clothing, and her skin was tanned and blistered with the sun'.[52] As the crew walked past Thompson/Giom, she is supposed to have called out, 'I am a white woman, why do you leave me?'[53]

Victoria K Haskins has rightly noted that Thompson's experiences with the Kuarareg have been 'submerged beneath the much more sensational story of her predecessor, Eliza Fraser ....'[54] In fact, Thompson's own account of her cohabitation is generally taken to be the complete opposite of Fraser's: calm, perceptive and informative. 'Although perfectly illiterate', MacGillivray writes, 'Mrs Thomson [*sic*] had made good use of her powers of observation, and evinced much shrewdness in her remarks upon various subjects connected with her residence among the blacks, joined to great willingness to communicate any information which she possessed'.[55]

Thompson also talked at length to Oswald Brierly, who interviewed her and read his transcriptions back to her for her approval. She spoke, he noted, 'in the manner of a person just waking up from a deep sleep and had not had time to collect her ideas':[56] recalling the Rip Van Winkle sense of emerging from a 'dreaming delusion' attributed to Buckley when he eventually returned to the colony. But she also provided detailed ethnographic insights, to do with her experiences of daily life, relations with other people, the work she undertook, the children she helped care for and so on. She affectionately described the people she lived with, offering details about their individual personalities and characteristics. Brierly is drawn to a moment when an Aboriginal elder, Sallalli, sits with her, 'talking in such kind tones to the white woman, calling her his child'.[57] 'There is something so calm and good about the old man', he observes. This is, overall, a benign cohabitation adventure, with none of the trauma, racism and melodrama associated with Fraser. It also isn't really a captivity narrative, even though the chapter title in MacGillivray's journals reads 'RESCUE A WHITE WOMAN FROM CAPTIVITY AMONG THE NATIVES'. It seems instead, as Haskins and Maynard suggest, that 'Thompson was treated with the greatest kindness and love by the Islanders'.[58]

In her interviews with Brierly, Thompson mentions a white man who had been living for a number of years on Badu Island, north of Muralag/Prince of Wales Island in the Torres Strait. 'He calls himself Gienow,' she says; 'The natives call him Weenie. He was [ship]wrecked ... he is a tall, middle-aged man. He is quite happy with the Blacks and does not care about leaving them'.[59] For MacGillivray, this white man became 'the most important person in the tribe, having gained an ascendancy by procuring the death of his principal enemies and intimidating others'.[60] He thinks Weenie must have been a convict who absconded from Norfolk Island; his character, he concludes, is a 'compound of villainy and cunning, in addition to the ferocity and headstrong passions of a thorough savage'.[61]

Thompson herself never seems to have used the term *savage* to describe the Kaurareg, in sharp contrast to Fraser on K'gari. MacGillivray, on the other hand, inverts the conventional colonial logic of this racist term by applying it to a white man. It seems as if Weenie is an example of a castaway cohabitant who has retreated as a far from colonisation as it is possible to get. This is his adventure; he is never 'rescued' and never returns, and barely registers in the colonial record.

~

In their fascinating book *Living with the Locals*, Haskins and Maynard look at what they call the 'Aboriginal lives' of thirteen white colonials, including Wilson, Buckley, Fraser and Thompson. Two other cases they discuss can be mentioned here. James Morrill was around twenty-two years old in 1846 when his ship, the *Peruvian*, was wrecked off the coast of Queensland. A small group survived on a raft for forty-two days, eventually washed up on the shores of Cape Cleveland, south of Townsville (Bindal and Wulgurukaba Country), where Birri-gubba people took them in and 'nursed [them] back to health'.[62] Morrill lived with groups of Birri-gubba for seventeen years and was treated with great kindness. But the stark reality of colonisation's rapid expansion provoked his now-famous reaction to the sight of two white stockmen in January 1863, 'Don't shoot, mates, I'm a British object!'.[63] In Queensland by this time, as Haskins and Maynard note, '[t]he killing times in the region had well and truly begun'.[64] Clearly, Morrill was well aware of colonisation as an utterly destructive force for Aboriginal people and gave his companions this dire warning: 'I told them the white men had come to take their land away'.[65]

Morrill was always proximate to colonisation and the fraught nature of the colonial frontier. But another young man—who also lived with Aboriginal people for seventeen years—was more remote from white encroachment and this made for a far different experience. Narcisse Pelletier was around fourteen years old when he left Marseilles in 1857, as a cabin boy on Captain Emmanuel Pinard's trading ship, the *Saint-Paul*. On its way from Hong Kong to New South Wales—with Chinese goldfields workers on board—the ship was wrecked on a reef near Rossel Island. With Pinard, Pelletier was part of a small crew that made a 1200-kilometre journey to Cape York, where the young cabin boy was casually abandoned. Like Morrill, he was nursed back to health, (in this case) by Uutaalnganu people, remaining with them until he was eventually picked up by a pearler, the *John Bell*, in April 1875. When Pelletier returned to France, his experiences were published by a doctor and scholar from Nantes, Constant Merland, as *Dix-Sept Ans Chez Les Sauvages: The Adventures of Narcisse Pelletier* (1876).

In her meticulous commentary on this narrative, Stephanie Anderson (like Fullagar, above) glosses the word *sauvage*: it reflects the prevailing discourse of the ethnographic moment, she notes, but it was 'less likely to be used in French anthropological circles ... than *les naturels* ("the natives") or *les indigenes* ("the indigenes") ... [or] *les Australiens* ("*the Australians*")'.[66] Merland's record of Pelletier's cohabitation presented ethnographic details, but it was also a colonial adventure narrative—and the term's connotations of wildness and barbarity were a key component of the genre's conventions. On the other hand, both Pelletier and Morrill were transformed by their cohabitation, a prolonged living arrangement that seemed to involve mutual affection and trust. Their experiences invert the logic of the colonial captivity narrative: they are *rescued* by Aboriginal people (not captured) and they're both ambivalent about leaving the people they've lived with to return to the colony so many years later.

The captivity narrative itself, as we have seen, can license a Manichean racism that relies on an almost unbreachable sense of distance from the colony/home: where white men and women end up in communities that seem, to them, far removed, and vastly different, from the only world they have known. This means that the colonial captivity narrative doesn't really register colonisation. It isn't that white cohabitants 'forget' about colonisation, as we saw with absconding convicts like Buckley or Davis/Duramboi and Bracewell/Wandi. Rather, it can seem as if colonisation has forgotten about *them*. The 'rescue' is a reminder that it hasn't: it tells us that colonisation eventually brings (almost) everyone back into its fold.

It also tells us that colonisation is always much closer to the captivity narrative than it pretends. William Jackman's *The Australian Captive; or, an authentic narrative of fifteen years in the life of William Jackman* (1853) is a good example of exactly this kind of pretence. Jackman was born in Devonshire in December 1821. Like so many colonial adventure narratives, his story begins when he goes to sea as a boy, eventually finding work on the convict ship *John Barry*, which arrived at Warrane/Sydney Cove in January 1836. Sailing on to Van Diemen's Land, Jackman argues with the captain and decides to abscond, heading into the bush. With the authorities in pursuit, he insists: 'I have my freedom, and I mean to maintain it'.[67] In April 1837 he boards the *Carib*, a (possibly fictitious) whaler, which is wrecked in a storm on the Nuyts Archipelago, off the coast of Tjutjuna/Ceduna in South Australia. Wirangu people approach him, holding spears; they strip him of his clothes and lead him through the bush to their huts. Jackman is frightened and thinks the Wirangu are cannibals. He has a Hobbesian view of them as 'a belligerent people', violent, superstitious, 'in a state of unceasing war'.[68] Eventually, he is picked up by a ship, the *Camilla*, and identified as the 'man who had been cast away on the coast, seventeen or eighteen months before'.[69] Later, Jackman sails to Canton; he goes whaling in the Pacific; and even joins the crew of a slave ship (a 'shameful and abominable transaction').[70] He ends up in New York in 1847.

The Australian Captive was published in the United States, transcribed and introduced by the Rev. Israel Chamberlayne, a New York-based Methodist Episcopal minister. As with Eliza Fraser's narrative, Jackman's was intended for an American readership: the Wirangu huts are 'wigwams', etc. But Chamberlayne (like Jackman?) seems unaware of Fraser's 1837 publication. 'The "Australian Captive" is believed to be a new character', he writes in his 1851 Preface to the narrative. 'If any other civilised man has returned from a forced and lengthened residence among the Anthropophagi of New Holland, and told the story of what he saw and suffered among them, the writer of this book has no knowledge of it'.[71] This is a colonial captivity narrative that wants to be the first of its kind. But how credible is it? Despite the 'authentic narrative' of the subtitle, Chamberlayne worries about how true Jackman's chronicle might actually be. It is, he notes, 'impossible to bring [the narrative's details] to the test of any known authorities'.[72] The problem here is not just to do with demonstrable truth, but with what it takes to produce a good colonial adventure narrative. 'Had the writer entered on his humble labor with the license of the fictionist', he says; 'had he even felt at liberty to *mend* the record, it had certainly issued in a very different, and, possibly, a much more engaging relation'.[73] Here, fiction ('mending the record') is a virtue for the adventure narrative; this is the opposite of the ship's journal, which, as we have seen, valued truth and credibility above all else. Chamberlayne wants Jackman's narrative to have some scientific value, especially in terms of its ethnographic and geographical details. But he also sees New Holland as somehow impervious to validation, a place that—for the adventure narrative to thrive—needs to remain uncharted and opaque (*incognita*) for as long as possible. As he puts it, 'Its extent considered ... there is, probably, no country on the globe, not even Africa, of which so little is known, and of which that little is liable to juster imputations of inaccuracy'.[74]

The end of the nineteenth century saw the publication of two late colonial cohabitation fantasies that went on to exploit this sense that the remotest parts of Australia were, even at this time, still beyond the realm of verifiable fact. Henri Louis Grin (or Grien) was born in Gressy, Switzerland, in 1847. He went to England and later emigrated to Western Australia, briefly holding a position as a domestic servant for the governor, Sir WC Robinson, in the mid-1870s. Working in various jobs, he eventually bought a pearling cutter, *Ada*, which went missing in early 1877. In 1880 he turned up in Warrane/Sydney, where he married Eliza Ravenscroft and started a family. He deserted his wife and children in 1897, and made his way to New Zealand and then to London. Here, Grin visited the well-known politician and journalist Sir John Henniker Heaton (who had spent around twenty years in New South Wales), announcing that 'he was LOUIS DE ROUGEMONT —the hero of the most remarkable adventures a man ever lived to tell'.[75] He claimed to have been a castaway in and around the Cambridge Gulf on the northern coast of Western Australia—on Balanggarra Country—living with Aboriginal people there for over thirty years.

Heaton introduced Grin/de Rougemont to William Fitzgerald, the editor of George Newnes's *Wide World Magazine*, a monthly periodical that celebrated the global (or imperial) reach of real-life exploration and discovery stories. 'There will be no fiction in the Magazine,' its opening editorial declared, 'but yet it will contain stories of weird adventure, more thrilling than any conceived by the novelist in his wildest flights'.[76] Fitzgerald published the first instalment of 'The Adventures of Louis de Rougemont; being a narrative of the most amazing experiences a man ever lived to tell' in September 1898. 'The narrative is taken down verbatim from M. de Rougemont's lips', he wrote, 'and apart from all outside authorities and experts, we have absolutely satisfied ourselves as to M. de Rougemont's accuracy in every minute particular'.[77] Newnes and Fitzgerald had such confidence in the truth of his narrative that they published it as a book in 1899. By this time, Grin/de Rougemont had become a notable celebrity and public speaker, 'the most discussed man in all Europe'.[78]

The Adventures of Louis de Rougemont is an outrageously preposterous account of cohabitation with Aboriginal people, even by the wildest standards of colonial adventure. De Rougemont's pearling boat is attacked by a giant octopus; there are tidal waves and hurricanes, rat plagues and locust plagues, a 'fish storm' (whitebait), and a snake pit; at one point, he rides on the back of a giant turtle. He takes an Aboriginal wife, Yamba, to whom his book is dedicated, and they have children. Later on, he rescues two 'extremely pretty' white teenage girls named Blanche and Gladys Rogers, who had been claimed from a shipwreck by a 'magnificently formed savage' and kept prisoner.[79] This is de Rougemont's own captivity narrative, which sees him as the heroic rescuer, although the girls later drown. Parts of the narrative intersect at the edge of actual events: for example, he meets Alfred Gibson, an explorer who joined Ernest Giles's expeditions into Western Australia in the early 1870s and who had disappeared without a trace. Endlessly congratulating himself for his achievements—and claiming to have been something close to a 'god' to the Aboriginal people he lives with—this is the outpouring of a massive colonial ego.

Despite the assurances of the *Wide World Magazine* and various members of the scientific community (such as Alfred Russel Wallace, the renowned naturalist/explorer), readers soon began to doubt the truth of de Rougemont's extraordinary experiences. By the end of October 1898, Melbourne's *Leader* was already proclaiming the whole thing 'a magnificent hoax' with 'no pretension to realistic accuracy'.[80] London's *Daily Chronicle* put together an exposé after the *Wide World Magazine*'s first instalment, holding what came to be called 'the trial of M. Louis de Rougemont'.[81] Louis Becke (whom we met in the Introduction) was in London at this time, and was called upon to question Grin/de Rougemont, presumably on the basis of his own knowledge of remote parts of Australia. Becke especially wondered about the rescue of the two girls: 'how is it that no one in Australia has, to my knowledge, heard of such a rescue? The feat ought to have made M. de Rougemont a hero in my country. We all know about Mrs Fraser and William Buckley and Morris [*sic*], and one Louis Pellatier [*sic*], and their captivity among the blacks; but we know nothing of the two English girls'.[82]

The *Daily Chronicle* went on to publish a full-length account of their investigations, *Grien on Rougemont; or the story of a modern Robinson Crusoe* (1898), with illustrations by *Bulletin* satirical artist Phil May and a sketch that lampooned Fitzgerald for his gullibility. The authors wrote: 'we thought that this history of his disappearance ... *might* have meant a modest residence among the blacks. But we are now satisfied that he never lived among them at all, unless it was as sojourners on the frontier of Australian civilisation do live in touch with natives from time to time, so as to pick up a certain scrappy knowledge of their ways'.[83] The *Daily Chronicle* also noted that Grin/de Rougemont's ethnographic information had nothing to do with the region he claimed to live in: 'the incidents of native life he talks of, so far as they are possible at all, are mainly a jumble of names and things taken with heedless promiscuity from North Queensland, the New Hebrides, and other regions, whose native habits have nothing in common with the Cambridge Gulf or with one another'.[84] In Warrane/Sydney, his estranged wife and children recognised him as Grin from his publicity photographs. Discredited as an imposter and a fraud, the newspapers began to describe Grin/de Rougemont as 'a modern Munchausen.'[85] This was, of course, a reference to Rudolph Erich Raspe's *The Surprising Adventures of the Renowned Baron Munchausen, Containing Singular Travels, Campaigns, Voyages, and Adventures* (1785), a fantasy that sees its deluded protagonist travel to distant places (even to the moon), welcome and triumphant wherever he goes.

The second cohabitation fantasy is much darker and also much closer to some stark colonial realities. William H Willshire had joined the South Australian police force in 1878; by the early 1880s he was leading punitive expeditions against Arrernte people in the Northern Territory, helping to secure land for cattle pastoralists. As head of a group of native police, Willshire set up stations at Heavitree Gap (which would later become Mparntwe/Alice Springs) and to the west at Boggy Creek in the mid-1880s, violently policing ('pacifying') the frontier. 'By his own admission', Amanda Nettelbeck and Robert Foster write in their book on Willshire, *In the Name of the Law* (2007), he 'shot dead innumerable Aboriginal people in the course of his patrols in the Interior'.[86]

Willshire was indeed a brutal killer of Aboriginal people, but he also promoted himself as an expert on Arrernte languages, politics and beliefs. His first book, *The Aborigines of Central Australia* (1888), was a work of amateur pseudo-ethnography that drew on his actual experiences with local communities. In February 1891 Willshire took some native police down to Tempe Downs, seeking out Matuntara people in response to pastoralists' complaints of cattle spearing and as payback for the killing of the father of one of his Aboriginal trackers.[87] Two Arrernte men were shot dead in their camp. Soon afterwards, Willshire was arrested by Francis J Gillen, who at the time was a magistrate and Aboriginal sub-protector.[88] Willshire was in fact the first police officer in the colonies to be charged with the murder of Aboriginal people. He was brought to trial in Port Augusta, where he was defended by the conservative lawyer (and twice premier of South Australia) Sir John Downer, with bail provided by local cattlemen. In the event, Willshire was acquitted; but the trial undermined his confidence in colonial justice, and derailed his assumption that he was its sanctioned agent and enforcer. In response to all this, he wrote a deliriously racist erotic fantasy about a white man living and travelling with Arrernte people, *A Thrilling Tale of Real Life in the Wilds of Australia* (1895).

This short piece of writing does two contradictory things. It wants to say that colonisation is increasingly impacting the lives of Aboriginal people in the Northern Territory, with the Arrernte anxious about 'white intruders ... strangers in their country'.[89] But it also sees the north as an Arcadian place that colonisation hasn't yet touched, an 'Austral paradise' with 'boundless hills and forests' and 'beautiful meadows'.[90] *A Thrilling Tale* is lovingly dedicated to a character called Chillberta, who may have been modelled on an Arrernte woman Willshire was involved with. The narrative mixes fantasy and memoir, with Chillberta giving the narrator/Willshire an Arrernte name, Oleara, and ushering him into the private domains of Arrernte cultural life. Oleara turns out to be infatuated with Arrernte women, who, he imagines, are all sexually attracted to him—although he remains resolutely 'chaste'.

This is an Edenic colonial fantasy that sees Arrernte women ('Australia's dusky daughters') as simultaneously innocent and promiscuous, free from the social constraints and moral strictures of western religion. (The Hermannsburg mission was not far away; Willshire often clashed with the missionaries.) Oleara/Willshire 'roams' with Chillberta and the Arrernte for a while, and then, without explanation, decides to leave and return to the colony. Arrested for the murder of two Aboriginal men, he then turns on the Arrernte, venting his hatred in conventionally racist terms ('savages', 'thieving blacks', etc). The fantasy comes to an end at this point, and the rest of the book is a series of press cuttings, complaints from various supporters about his arrest, character testimonies ('a man whose only fault was, that he served his country too well!') and so on.[91] Willshire's trial and acquittal in Kurdnatta/Port Augusta lead to more expressions of contempt for Aboriginal people, the blame falling on the two murdered Arrernte men. The book's earlier cohabitation fantasy seems like another Rip Van Winkle episode, where the narrator's dreams of sexual freedom and shared cultural experience are finally shut down by an unwavering assertion of colonial power and righteousness. There is no more 'roaming' with Aboriginal people here. Colonisation in this account now follows a straight path towards its own future; it is a resolutely single-minded (ad)venture. As one correspondent in Willshire's book chillingly puts it, 'We whites are here for a purpose ....'[92]

CHAPTER 4

Bushrangers, etc

IT IS NOW reasonably well known that the first bushranger in the colonies was of African descent: a convict named John Caesar, who had been transported from England with the First Fleet on the convict ship *Alexander*. In the 1980s historians such as Mollie Gillen and Ian Duffield began to pay attention to the dozen or so people of colour transported to Australia at this time from Africa and the Americas; providing often speculative details about their backgrounds (emancipated or runaway slaves, for example) and what happened to them afterwards.[1] As Duffield notes, *An Account of the English Colony of New South Wales* by the colony's judge advocate, David Collins, is one of the few primary sources of information about 'Black Caesar', as he was then known.[2] A head count in May 1789 of convicts from the First Fleet showed that one of them was missing. Caesar, 'an incorrigibly stubborn black', Collins writes, 'had absconded a few days before ... and taken to the woods'.[3] It had initially seemed as if Caesar was 'the hardest working convict in the country; his frame was muscular and well calculated for hard labour'.[4] But when he was captured and returned to the colony, he taunted the authorities and was openly insubordinate: 'He was such a wretch, and so indifferent about meeting death, that he declared while in confinement, that if he should be hanged, he would create a laugh before he was turned off, by playing off some trick upon the executioner'.[5]

Over the next few years, Caesar absconded a number of times, raiding settler properties. By the end of 1795 Collins appears almost to have given up on him: 'A savage of a darker hue, and still as far removed from civilisation, black Caesar once more fled from honest labour to the woods, there to subsist by robbing the settlers. It was, however, reported that he had done one meritorious action, killing Pe-mul-wuy ...'[6] Pemulwuy was a Bidjigal (Bidgigal) man, who had led Aboriginal guerrilla resistance in and around Botany Bay. The news that he had been killed turned out to be false. Even so, it gave Caesar the kind of liminal role in the colony that we saw with James Wilson in Chapter 3—sometimes living outside and against its jurisdiction, while at other times doing its colonising work. The New South Wales governor, John Hunter, finally offered a reward of 5 gallons of rum for Caesar's capture or death. An ex-convict, John Winbow (or Wimbow),[7] found Caesar's 'haunt' in February 1796 and killed him. 'This ended a man', Collins wrote, letting his racist contempt flow, 'who certainly, during his life, could never have been estimated at one remove above the brute, and who had given more trouble than any other convict in the settlement'.[8]

Ian Duffield's comments on Black Caesar follow his discussion of the only colonial Australian novel with an 'Afro-Black' bushranger protagonist: Alexander Harris's *The Emigrant Family* (1849), reprinted in 1852 as *Martin Beck; or The Story of an Australian Settler*. Beck is a 'fine and rather handsome man', with 'all the fire of Africa in his veins'.[9] Like Caesar, he works hard and initially seems trustworthy, but he secretly steals cattle and money from local settlers. When he is discovered, he flees to Gulu-Mada/the Blue Mountains and becomes a notorious bushranger, known to the authorities as Black Beck. The novel's choice of a protagonist of African descent suggests that Harris may well have been aware of Collins's earlier accounts of Black Caesar. For Duffield, Caesar was New South Wales's 'original proto-bushranger', a claim repeated in more recent commentaries on this figure.[10] In fact, Collins never used the term 'bushranger' to describe him. But in just a few years' time, it appears as if it is in full circulation. The first mention of it in colonial media is a report in the *Sydney Gazette and New South Wales Advertiser* that on 12 February 1805 'a cart was stopped between [Sydney] and Hawkesbury, by three men whose appearance sanctioned the suspicion of their being bush-rangers. They had been previously observed lurking about the Ponds [north of Parramatta] by a carrier, who passed unmolested ....'[11]

Bushrangers are already a recognisable character type here, and they threaten some people, it seems, but not others. The *Sydney Gazette* during this time is full of accounts of bushrangers (always hyphenated in these early reports) either at large, being caught, coming to trial, or being punished, usually with prolonged floggings. Like Collins with Caesar, the newspaper couldn't quite understand why people would choose to leave the colony and abscond into the bush, living a life defined by risk and hardship, constantly pursued by soldiers and threatened with arrest. To be a bush-ranger from this perspective was to be de-ranged: from the French *déranger*, to disturb, to annoy, but also (from the Old French *desrengier*) 'to throw into disorder', to go mad. The arrest of a bush-ranger named John Bellar in March 1806 led the *Sydney Gazette* to reflect at extraordinary length on 'the extreme mental anxiety of a man who banishes himself from society for the precarious dependency afforded by the woods'.[12] This is where we find the cultural logics of the bushranger adventure: as a narrative of (self-)banishment, where someone chooses a 'precarious' life in the woods over the security of home and colony, and as a consequence can seem from the colony's point of view to have completely taken leave of their senses.

The first bushranger adventure narrative to be published in the colonies was a biography, *Michael Howe, the Last and Worst of the Bush Rangers of Van Diemen's Land*, compiled and printed early in 1819 by Andrew Bent, the founding editor of the *Hobart Town Gazette*.[13] Like John Caesar, Howe was a transported convict, arriving in Van Diemen's Land on the *Indefatigable* in October 1812. Assigned to work for a former superintendent of convicts, he soon 'eloped into the bush' (as Bent's pamphlet puts it) and joined a bushranger gang led by John Whitehead. Howe became leader of the gang when Whitehead was killed, and effectively waged a war on the colony, declaring himself 'Lieutenant-Governor of the Woods'. This is closer to insurrection than insubordination; it helps explain why *Michael Howe* likens its protagonist to the Jamaican resistance fighter known as Three-fingered Jack (Jack Mansong), a runaway slave and folk hero 'who was so long the terror of the peaceable settlers in the plantations'.[14]

James Boyce suggests that around a hundred bushrangers were in Howe's gang between 1815 and 1818, with 'the British authorities in Van Diemen's Land ... engaged in what amounted to a civil war'.[15] Controlling many of the colony's resources and ruining the livelihoods of prominent settlers, Howe was, as Boyce suggests, 'the only Australian bushranger to pose a genuine alternative to the colonial government's political authority'.[16] Lieutenant-Governor Thomas Davey had offered an amnesty to the bushrangers in December 1814, but it wasn't successful, so he followed up with a declaration of martial law. At some point in late 1816, Howe and ten bushrangers signed a letter written in blood to Davey, wanting a better deal both for themselves and the colony's settlers. 'We will be watching', they write, in an escalating series of threats; 'Likewise you Must Not think to Catch Hold Birds with Chaff ... We have Weighed Well Within Our Own Brests the Consequence Which Will Attend to those Circumstances Therefore I Would Have you Do the same for the Good of the Peacable and Well Disposed Inhabitants of the Territorys of this Land'.[17] With its evocative use of an old saying (that the wise cannot be deceived), this is a bushranger's complaint aimed directly at the colony's administrative powers that also claims the right to speak on behalf of ordinary people. It is surely a precursor to Ned Kelly's famous *Jerilderie Letter* (1879), which we'll discuss below.

Bent's *Michael Howe* concentrates all of the action and events in this bushranger's turbulent life into a short rise-and-fall narrative that sees Howe initially successful, and then increasingly desperate and alone. Two young Aboriginal women had joined the bushrangers. Howe was in a relationship with one of them: a mouhenneener woman known as Mary Cockerill or 'Black Mary', who had been taken in as domestic help by a settler family (possibly as a stolen child). Mary Cockerill was the first female Aboriginal bushranger; her knowledge of Country no doubt helped Howe survive for as long as he did, and she joined him on his raids. Pursued by soldiers near Jericho, north of nipaluna/Hobart, Howe shot Mary in a callous act of self-preservation when she 'was unable to keep pace with him in his flight'.[18] Mary then became an informant and a 'native guide' for the soldiers, helping them to track the bushranger. In September 1817 William Sorell (who had replaced Davey as lieutenant-governor) offered a reward of 100 guineas for Howe's capture. With other bushrangers from the gang now caught (and, in some cases, executed), this 'most hardened and sanguinary' bushranger was now, Bent's pamphlet tell us, 'cut off from association with man', buried in 'unknown and inaccessible parts of the woods'.[19]

Cast out of the colony, Howe is effectively alienated from humanity itself, 'standing opposed to all mankind'.[20] At one point, a settler finds his abandoned belongings and makes a striking discovery: 'In his knapsack was found a sort of journal of dreams; which shew strongly the distressed state of his mind, and some tincture of superstition'.[21] The 'little book of kangaroo skin, written in kangaroo blood' suggests the extent of Howe's particular derangement, alongside some rather touching, conventional aspirations: for example, 'that he had always an idea of settling in the woods' in a place with a garden full of fruits and flowers.[22] When he was finally killed—in October 1818—Howe 'wore ... a dress made of kangaroo skins ... and presented an altogether terrific appearance'.[23] The moralising narrative regards his death as the authorised execution of a 'monster' that gave the settlers 'an inconceivable degree of satisfaction'.[24]

Four copies of Bent's *Michael Howe* apparently made it to Britain. One of them was sent by Lachlan Macquarie, the governor of New South Wales, to Sir Walter Scott, and can still be found in his library at Abbotsford in Scotland.[25] Scott was one of the founders of the *Quarterly Review*; in May 1820 the journal published a review of *Michael Howe*, attributed at least in part to the ambitious Warrane/Sydney magistrate Barron Field. The review isn't surprised to find that the earliest literature from Van Diemen's Land paradoxically turns out to consist of 'last dying speeches and confessions'.[26] The first book in the colony is already a last gasp, or so it seems. Field had published his own book, *First Fruits of Australian Poetry*, in the same year as Bent's *Michael Howe*, a collection of just two poems. *Michael Howe* is an adventure narrative about the 'last' colonial bushranger; but Field announces himself as the 'first' colonial poet and even makes a claim on adventure itself as a way of accounting for the literary journey he has taken. 'I first adventure', his epigraph tells us. 'Follow me who list; / And be the second Austral Harmonist'. The epigraph is adapted from the seventeenth century English satirist Joseph Hall: 'I first adventure, follow me who list, / And be the second English Satyrist'.[27]

Adventurers, as we have noted, always like to be the first to arrive. But the *Quarterly Review*'s account of Bent's *Michael*

Howe is 'happy to hear that these bush-rangers are at length exterminated': as if their own adventure is now at an end.[28] Bent's introductory note to *Michael Howe* had also spoken about 'the Extinction of Bush-Ranging'.[29] But bushranging began to flourish in the colonies; and even Howe had a productive cultural afterlife. In 1821 the *Hobart Town Gazette* noted the performance in April of a 'melo-drama' called *Michael Howe: the Terror of Van Diemen's Land*, at Royal Coburg Theatre (later, the Old Vic) in London.[30] It was written by a now-forgotten Anglo–American dramatist, John H Amherst, and was in fact the first play about life (and death) in Van Diemen's Land.[31] A much more successful English playwright, William Thomas Moncrieff, went on to revive Michael Howe's career in a musical drama, *Van Diemen's Land*, first produced at the Surrey Theatre in February 1830.

The figure of the bushranger began to proliferate in cultural works around this time, with more early plays, as well as poetry, ballads, stories, novels and so on. The Scottish-born David Burn had lived for a while on his mother's extensive property, Ellangowan, near Hamilton, in Van Diemen's Land; she was the first woman to be granted land in that colony. Burn was an advocate for colonisation and colonial development, regarding the island's wilderness as 'a worthless waste, until the genius and industry of man converts and fits them for the welfare and enjoyment of his kind'.[32] His play *The Bushrangers* was staged in Edinburgh in 1829, and was based on the life of the Vandemonian Matthew Brady, a 'gentleman bushranger', who in 1824 had notoriously overpowered an entire town, Sorell, locking soldiers in the local gaol.

Brady was captured and hanged in May 1826. A year later, Andrew Bent published an amusing piece of satirical verse, *The Van Diemen's Land Warriors, or the Heroes of Cornwall*, by 'Pindar Juvenal'. (The identity of the author is not known for certain.) A baker from Cornwall, a small town in the north-east of lutruwita/Tasmania, urges a group of local tradespeople—a cobbler, a tailor, a blacksmith, a pastry cook, a hatter, etc—to take up arms, and go in pursuit of Brady and his gang. But the bushranger is a step ahead of them. He captures the men, threatens them with a flogging, and then decides to take their trousers instead, sending them back to Launceston, humiliated. Returning home, the locals realise that they are simply not cut out for adventure:

In such a glaring dishabille, alas!
Through streets of Launceston compelled to pass,
The girls and women vowed t'was monstrous rude
For men to walk about the town so nude;
While every ragged little urchin screeches,
Pray what's the price of buck-*skin* breeches?

At last they gladly each arrive once more
Safely within his own respective door,
Resolved no more in search of fame to roam
To mind his business, and stay at home.[33]

The bushranger is a folk hero here, generous of spirit, full of mischievous humour. A number of bushrangers made their way into ballads that sang their praises more overtly: like the anonymous (and difficult to date) 'The Wild Colonial Boy' and 'Bold Jack Donohue', both of which celebrated the rebellious spirit of the Irish-born bushranger John Donahue (or Donahoe, or Donohoe), who roamed around much of New South Wales in the 1820s. When Donahue was shot and killed by mounted police in September 1830, the *Sydney Gazette* gave him a predictably damning epitaph, a counterpoint to the more upbeat sentiments of the ballads: 'Thus is the Colony rid of one of the most dangerous spirits that ever infested it, and happy would it be were those of a like disposition to take warning by his awful fate'.[34]

In May 1834 a young Charles Harpur (he was twenty-one) brought 'a tragedy composed in blank verse' about Donohue into the offices of the *Sydney Monitor*.[35] The newspaper didn't much like the blank verse, but it went on to serialise extracts from Harpur's playscript in February the following year. Later on, Harpur renamed the bushranger 'Stalwart' and called his play *The Bushrangers*, publishing it in 1853 with some of his best-known poetry. Here, Donohoe/Stalwart is the resentful villain of a melodrama, full of passionate declarations ('I have talked / My spirit into such a blaze!').[36] A tailor and a shoemaker provide some comic relief, perhaps a nod to the hapless characters in *The Van Diemen's Land Warriors*. But Harpur's play is the opposite of the boisterous bushranger ballads mentioned above. Stalwart is a cold-blooded murderer; when he is finally shot and killed, he imagines he is dragged down to Hell.

There may be some structural affinities between Aboriginal resistance fighters and Aboriginal bushrangers. We wouldn't want the latter term to diminish the capacity and urgency of the former in any way; but it is possible that bushranging gave some Aboriginal participants access to levels of resistance that might otherwise have been unavailable to them. When Mary Cockerill joined Michael Howe's gang, she was an armed participant in raids on settler properties. From the colony's perspective, her identity had radically shifted over time: from that of a colonial family's domestic servant (taken from, or having left, her community), to a bushranger and bushranger's companion, and, finally (to the colony's relief), a tracker and informant with an excellent 'knowledge of the country'.[37] Her identity seems to have been fluid, and liminal, a sequence of varying relations to the sheer fact of colonisation; sometimes working for it, sometimes militantly against it, depending on her circumstances.

Another female Aboriginal bushranger, Mary Ann Bugg—whose partner from around 1863 to1867 was Frederick Ward, alias Captain Thunderbolt—is also worth mentioning here. With a Worimi mother (from country north of Mulubinba/Newcastle) and a white ex-convict father, Bugg was educated in Warrane/Sydney and had been in long-term relationships with settler farmers before she met Ward. Meg Foster discusses Bugg in her book about five non-white bushrangers from the second half of the nineteenth century, *Boundary Crossers* (2022). Bugg, she notes, was more than just Ward's companion: 'She accompanied him around the colony, acting as his scout, informer, lover, and confidante. She provided food and shelter, bore him three children, and at the time, many colonists alleged that she took part in the robberies herself'.[38] Bugg was not an Aboriginal resistance fighter, but she allows Foster to think about the relationship between Aboriginal warfare and bushranging more generally. Aboriginal raids on settlers, as she puts it, were 'akin to bushranging';[39] and 'the collusion between Aboriginal people and white bushrangers ... made the violence [against settlers] all the more threatening'.[40] She adds, 'This is not to say that Aboriginal warfare and bushranging were the same, but that their intersections shaped the contours of Mary Ann's life'.[41]

In May 1805 the *Sydney Gazette* wrote about the Dharug resistance fighter Pemulway's son, Tedbury (or Tjedboro), who was showing 'propensities of the most diabolical complexion'. At one point, Tedbury was taken by a party of settlers to a place where some weapons used to kill local stockmen were hidden. Nearby, they met another Dharug man 'called Bush Muschetta, [who] saluted them in good English, and declaring a determination to continue their rapacities, made off'.[42] Bush Muschetta—or Musquito, as he was known in the colony—was an Aboriginal resistance fighter from Gai-Maraigal Country. He was active around Dyarubbin/the Hawkesbury River districts during this time, raiding settler properties but also engaging in warfare with other Aboriginal groups in the region.[43] Local trackers helped to capture Musquito, who was taken to Parramatta Gaol and exchanged for Tedbury. A report in the *Sydney Gazette* in early August 1805 noted that Musquito and another Dharug man, Toula or Toulgra (known to the colony as 'Bulldog'), had tried to escape, maintaining a 'spirit of destruction' by threatening 'to set fire to the building, and destroy every white man within it'.[44] Exiled to Norfolk Island as a convict labourer, Musquito remained there until 1813. He ended up in Van Diemen's Land, where he was drafted by the colony as a tracker, going in pursuit of (among others) Michael Howe and Mary Cockerill. Musquito also worked for Edward Lord, a controversial trader and grazier, who was said at the time to have been Van Diemen's Land's wealthiest man.

For various reasons—most likely because he was not permitted to return to Gai-Maraigal Country in New South Wales—Musquito absconded into the forests around Hobart Town, and joined a 'tame mob' or 'tame gang': that is, palawa people who had left or been taken away from their communities (for example, to work in settler households) and had then absconded from the colony. In this liminal, provisional space, we might identify Musquito as an Aboriginal bushranger. By the early 1820s, however, he had gone further afield, joining the paredarerme or Oyster Bay people, who had been raiding settler properties around the south-east coast. We would now regard Musquito as an Aboriginal resistance fighter (as he was in New South Wales), active in what were the early days of the Tasmanian War. The so-called Grindstone Bay attack in November 1823—where two stock-keepers were killed—saw Musquito and a young palawa man known as Black Jack vigorously pursued by colonial authorities. The two men were blamed for other, subsequent attacks on settlers, too. As Naomi Parry suggests, a 'certain hysteria' was developing in the colony, which had 'attributed the sudden outbreak of violence to the influence of Musquito'—even though there was often little evidence of his direct involvement.[45]

In August 1824 an Aboriginal teenager named Tegg or Teague, accompanied by two white men, found Musquito and shot at him 'on the promise of a reward from the Lieutenant Governor [George Arthur] in the event of his being successful'.[46] (Like Mary Cockerill, Tegg was probably taken in to domestic labour by settlers; he, too, became an Aboriginal bushranger for a short period of time.[47]) Recovering from his wounds in the Colonial Hospital, Musquito was brought to trial in December and found guilty of the murder of the two Grindstone Bay stock-keepers. Black Jack had also been caught and was found guilty of the murder of a settler from Sorell Plains. On 25 February 1825 Musquito, Black Jack and six bushrangers were hanged; Musquito is reported to have told his gaoler, 'Hanging no good for black fellow ... Very good for white fellow, for he used to it'.[48] The Tasmanian War was beginning to escalate around this time. Given his strong connections to paradareme people in particular, it's worth wondering if the executions of Musquito and Black Jack contributed to that escalation.

The Eton-educated Charles Rowcroft was a landowner and magistrate at Oatlands, about 60 kilometres inland from Oyster Bay. He had written to Governor Arthur 'pleading for military assistance because Musquito's band', as he put it, 'was "infesting" the district'.[49] It happened that around the time Musquito was brought to trial in Hobart Town, Rowcroft was also in court, facing a charge brought against him by Edward Lord for 'criminal conversation' (that is, adultery) with his wife, Maria. Rowcroft was found guilty and fined £100. Impoverished, he returned to England; Lord also returned to England, while Maria remained in Van Diemen's

Land and became a successful local businesswoman. Living in London, Rowcroft went on to publish a number of adventure novels in the 1840s and early 1850s. The first of these, *Tales of the Colonies; or, The Adventures of an Emigrant* (1843), presents Musquito as a striking, charismatic figure. The narrator, William Thornley, emigrates with his wife and children from Surrey, arriving in Van Diemen's Land in early 1817. He soon establishes a farm north of Hobart Town and keeps track of colonial developments in the district. In October 1818 Thornley mentions the death of the bushranger Michael Howe: 'This is a good riddance', he remarks.[50] The novel shifts to 1824, when news of more bushrangers in the colony makes Thornley feel 'uncomfortable and restless' about possible threats to his increasing wealth.[51] Aboriginal people are also actively resisting settler expansion, adding to his anxieties. This is where the novel introduces Musquito: 'At this time a native of Australia, by name Musquito, a tall and powerful man, had been committing many atrocities in Van Diemen's Land ... It was known that he was at the head of a mob of natives, consisting of about thirty; but we had no idea he was in this part of the island ....'[52] What worries Thornley most is the possibility that Musquito 'should join with the bushrangers', which 'might be more than we could cope with.'[53]

Tales of the Colonies is a tribute to the business of colonisation, and the wealth and opportunities it brings to hard-working settlers. But to be an adventure novel, it needed to (re-)create an environment full of risk and danger. At one point, Thornley gets lost in the bush and finds himself under attack by a group of palawa people with 'Musquito ... at their head'.[54] Not long afterwards, he faces off with another leader, the notorious bushranger Gypsey, who is being pursued by constables. Gypsey tells him about his daughter, Georgiana, and Thornley, overcome with sympathy, agrees to take care of her. When the police arrive, the bushranger leaps to his death over a precipice, taking a constable with him. In Hobart Town later on, Thornley is horrified to learn that Georgiana has been kidnapped by two white men, one of whom turns out to be Gypsey's brother. The men are then killed by Musquito and his mob, who take the girl to their camp. Thornley, a magistrate and some settlers go to the camp to try to retrieve her—giving full vent to their racist beliefs about savagery, treachery, cannibalism, etc, on the way. When they arrive, they recognise Musquito 'by his stature and bearing', 'distinguished by a black hat, with waistcoat and trousers'.[55] The settlers expect a hostile reception, given his reputation as 'the cruellest savage that ever tormented a colony'.[56] But instead, Thornley has 'the awkward feeling of having intruded on a gentleman's privacy without an invitation'.[57] This is the closest the novel gets to acknowledging settler incursions onto Aboriginal territory as troubling or problematic.

Musquito is hospitable, but the settlers wonder why he brought the bushranger's daughter to his camp. He explains that Gypsey is his 'brother': there is an expression of kinship here between a Dharug man in Van Diemen's Land and a white bushranger, both fighting their own wars with the colony. Georgiana runs into Thornley's arms, in a sentimental scene that might recall Eliza Fraser's rescue by John Graham, discussed in Chapter 3. The novel finishes with Musquito—at this point, only a few months before his real-life capture, trial and execution. He is mentioned just once more at the end of the novel, when—fourteen years later—Georgiana, now a wealthy married woman living in England, writes in a letter to Thornley, 'My husband says he should have liked to know Musquito, for he was a fine fellow for saving my life, and he says it was a shame to hang him; but the atrocities and murders that he committed are certainly very shocking'.[58] The letter reintroduces Musquito to the narrative right at the end, long after his death; it revives and redeems him (to a degree), while consigning him to a now-distant point in colonial frontier history. Finishing the letter, Thornley reflects on 'my busy and adventurous life' in those early days.[59] *Tales of the Colonies* celebrates adventure as a self-defining colonial settler experience, a necessary part of the process of dispossessing Aboriginal people, clearing the land and establishing secure, prosperous properties. But it also wants to say that the days of colonial adventure are now over: the 'risks' have been overcome, Aboriginal resistance fighters have been hanged and the bushrangers are all dead.

First person accounts of a bushranger's life are rare: there are very few bushranger memoirs or autobiographies. A couple of exceptions appeared in the 1870s, both of which presented themselves as adventure narratives. Born in County Wexford, Ireland, Martin Cash was transported to Warrane/Sydney (he had tried to shoot a romantic rival) in early 1828, on the convict ship *Marquis of Huntly*. Wanted for cattle stealing later on, Cash fled New South Wales for Van Diemen's Land; the first thing that caught his attention when he arrived there was a coffin containing the body of a hanged bushranger. His autobiography, *The Adventures of Martin Cash* (1870), is a breathless, rollicking account of his various escapades on the island with 'two desperate men' from New South Wales, Lawrence Kavanagh and George Jones. The gang roams through the forests ('A life in the woods for me!'), raiding property after property, with police and soldiers in constant pursuit. Captured at last and placed on a ship destined for Norfolk Island, someone hands him a sheet of paper with a ballad on it that celebrates Cash's Irishness and his courage: 'He's the bravest man that you could choose from Sydney men or Cockatoos, / And a gallant son of Erin, where the sprig of Shamrock grows'.[60]

Marcus Clarke had drawn on Cash's experiences at Norfolk Island in the mid-1840s, under the commandant Joseph Childs, for the last part of *His Natural Life*. At one point, Cash describes a mutiny and some killings by convicts, led by the ex-bushranger William Westwood, an otherwise 'quiet inoffensive man' who had been 'flogged, goaded, and tantalised till he was reduced to a lunatic and a savage'.[61] The penal colony's religious instructor, Thomas Rogers—the model for the Rev. Mr North in Clarke's novel, as we noted in Chapter 2—spent time with Westwood in his condemned cell and encouraged him to tell his life story. Westwood was hanged in October 1846. For some reason, Rogers didn't publish the notes he had taken until much later on, serialising Westwood's narrative (under the pseudonym 'Peutetre') in four weekly issues of the

Australasian in February 1879. As it happens, this was around the time that Ned Kelly and his gang were raiding Jerilderie in the Riverina region of New South Wales, just north of the Victorian border.

For Rogers, Westwood's narrative reveals 'the incidents and motives of a bushranger's life from a point of view from which it is seldom seen', offering an 'unadorned and straightforward tale of audacious bushranger adventure and privation, in which a young outlaw relates in his own way the incidents of his brigand career'.[62] Westwood was transported to Warrane/Sydney Cove on the *Mangles* in 1837. He soon absconded and was involved in numerous bail ups on the road. His robberies were audacious: in one, he holds up a wealthy settler's house, where a female servant wants to run off with him ('a faithful companion she was'); in another, he robs one of the magistrates who had sentenced him. At Port Arthur later on, he is flogged and put in solitary confinement. When he absconds again, he is given a ten-year sentence on Norfolk Island: this is where his autobiography comes to an end.

Ned Kelly's *Jerilderie Letter* is the third bushranger's autobiography worth noting here, the best-known example of a bushranger's unmediated voice recounting actual experiences. Kelly had already completed his manuscript by the time his gang got to Jerilderie, and he tried to get it published in the town's newspaper; but in fact, it wasn't published in its entirety until 1930. It can now be seen online in both its original form and as a typescript at the National Museum of Australia.[63] The *Letter* is a remarkable document, a fascinating account of Kelly's various battles with the police that escalates into a ranting diatribe against colonial authorities and the colonial state. Kelly both leaves home (that is his adventure) and remains close to home; the *Letter* itself oscillates around the Greta district (Wanaruah Country), where he grew up. It has often been discussed in detail,[64] but we can look at a passage here to appreciate the rhetorical force of Kelly's mode of expression, its vivid condemnation of the brutalities of the penal system, and the way he radicalises himself by insisting on his unbroken connection to Ireland—unlike the Irish colonial policeman in this opening line:

> A policeman who for a lazy loafing cowardly bilit [billet, at a police station] left the ash corner [i.e. the fireplace or hearth at home] deserted the shamrock, the emblem of true wit and beauty to serve under a flag and nation that has destroyed massacred and murdered their forefathers by the greatest of torture as rolling them down hill in spiked barrels pulling their toe and finger nails and on the wheel. And every torture imaginable more was transported to Van Diemen's Land to pine their young lives away in starvation and misery among tyrants worse than the promised hell itself all of true blood bone and beauty, that was not murdered on their own soil, or had fled to America or other countries bloom again another day, were doomed to Port McQuarie, Toweringgabbie [Toongabbie, north of Parramatta] Norfolk Island and Emu Plains And in those places of tyranny and condemnation many a blooming Irishman rather than subdue to the Saxon yoke, Were flogged to death and

> bravely died in servile chains but true to the shamrock and a credit to Paddys land.[65]

The language in this passage (and all through the *Letter*) is in some respects closer to poetry than to the 'unadorned' prose we might usually expect from a bushranger's autobiography. The phrase 'true wit and beauty' becomes the more alliterative 'true blood bone and beauty' soon afterwards, while 'bloom' is echoed in its opposite, 'doomed', and is then repeated as both a mild profanity and an expression of good health and promise in 'many a blooming Irishman'. Russel Ward's classic study *The Australian Legend* (1958)—which had talked at length about the bushranger as a folk hero—noted that this is also a passage where the *Letter* fleetingly turns into song. It reproduces (from Kelly's memory?) lines from a famous ballad, Francis MacNamara's 'Moreton Bay', where a convict sings, 'I have been a prisoner at Port Macquarie, at Norfolk Island and Emu Plains; / At Castle Hill and cursed Towngabbie—at all those places I've worked in chains'.[66] For Kelly, it is better to die in 'servile chains' and stay loyal to Ireland than serve the (English) colonial authorities: this is the passage's rhetorical act of insubordination.

The historian Mark McKenna has dismissed the *Letter* as 'aggressive' and 'belligerent', a 'shallow form of republicanism' without any real political purpose.[67] Certainly, it is not quite the declaration of civil war we saw sixty years earlier in Michael Howe's letter written in blood to Lieutenant-Governor Thomas Davey. But it works in a similar way, escalating its rhetoric in a last-gasp series of threats against the police who

Kelly hated so intensely. Those who support them, he suggests, should give their money instead to 'the poor of Greta district' (like Howe's 'Peacable and Well Disposed Inhabitants of the Territorys of this Land'). The powerful end of the *Jerilderie Letter* sees Kelly transformed from a bushranger wanted *by* the law to someone who imagines he *is* the law: this is his derangement. A lone voice in the wilderness at this point, he nevertheless promises retribution to the colony's authorities. By the end of the *Letter*, it is as if he has become a force of nature:

> do not attempt to reside in Victoria but as short a time as possible after reading this notice, neglect this and abide by the consequence which shall be worse than rust in wheat in Victoria or the drought of a dry season to the grasshoppers in New South Wales. I do not wish to give the order full force without giving timely warning but I am a Widow's Son, outlawed and my orders must be obeyed.[68]

~

As we have seen, even the earliest accounts of bushrangers in the colonies spoke confidently of their imminent 'extinction'. Bushrangers outlived this prediction, but—with one or two exceptions, such as Martin Cash (who retired as a respectable hat-maker in Van Diemen's Land)—their profession was invariably a fatal one and the colonies generally refused to let them live. The hanging of Ned Kelly at the Melbourne Gaol in

November 1880 suggested to many that 'the last of the bushrangers' had indeed finally departed. In George E Boxall's *History of the Australian Bushrangers* (1899), bushrangers surely couldn't be a part of the Federation that was soon to come. Like 'blackbirding' (see the Introduction), the adventure had to be consigned to the past as a historical curiosity specific to the colonies but out of place in the newly formed nation. Bushranging, as Boxall put it, 'was rather an excrescence on, than a development of, Australian character'.[69] The word *excrescence* suggests growth (like *development*), but of something abnormal or parasitical that would need to be surgically removed. For Boxall, the Kelly gang is 'the last epoch' of bushranging, which the colonies, as Federation drew closer, had 'purged away by the most drastic remedies'.[70] But the end of the Kelly gang also led to a sense that something had been lost, something that was indeed adventurous. 'Thus ended the last act', Boxall writes, 'in the great tragedy which had supplied almost the only feature of romance to Australian history'.[71]

Two of the best-known bushranger novels published in the last decades of the colonial period return to that 'last act'. They present the bushranger as an outlaw figure who must be resurrected—to confirm that link between the colonies and romance—but only in order to be put to rest all over again. 'Rolf Boldrewood's' (TA Browne's) *Robbery Under Arms* was serialised in the *Sydney Mail* in 1882 and 1883, just a couple of years after Kelly was hanged. It was published as a three-volume novel in London in 1888, and as a two-volume novel by Leipzig's Tauchnitz in 1889. That same year, it was also published as a revised single volume in Macmillan's Colonial Library. The novel capitalised on 'the rising tide of romance' across the Anglophone world, with 'multiple editions' in the United States;[72] and it went on to become an 'imperial bestseller'.[73]

But it wasn't about the present day. *Robbery Under Arms* is a historical novel set in the 1840s and 1850s. The model here is Sir Walter Scott, who had more or less invented historical adventure fiction with *Waverley* (1814): a novel that drew attention, as Peter Fritzsche writes, 'to the "just passed" quality of a still half-remembered age'.[74] Boldrewood was profoundly influenced by Scott. He got his pen name from a line in Scott's poem *Marmion* (1808) and named the first property he bought in the colonies, Squattlesea Mere in western Victoria (north of Port Fairy), after an estate in Lincolnshire owned by a character named Wildrake in Scott's novel *Woodstock* (1826). Scott's protagonists are often considered to be 'neutral' in relation to the politically passionate characters around them, which also meant they tended to survive the longest.[75] In Boldrewood's *Robbery Under Arms*, the protagonist and narrator is Dick Marston, the youngest son in a family of three children, with an Irish Catholic mother and a violent English ex-convict father (a Lincolnshire poacher). The Marstons are farmers, but the father and his sons soon go bushranging, leaving the mother and sister, Aileen, at home. Structurally, the novel is a bit like Kelly's *Jerilderie Letter*, with the bushrangers seeking their adventures elsewhere but never really breaking their family ties. When the novel begins, however, Dick is languishing in jail while his father, Ben, his brother, Jim, an Aboriginal companion and tracker named Warrigal, and the 'gentleman bushranger' Captain Starlight are all dead. So is the 'cruel, treacherous, unmanly' bushranger Dan Moran, based on the actual bushranger Dan Morgan, who was shot and killed in April 1865.[76] (In the revised 1889 Macmillan version, Moran and his gang are for some reason allowed to live, although Marston adds: 'Their time, like ours, was drawing short ...')[77]

Boldrewood knew about Dan Morgan and expected an attack from him early in 1864, as he made his way, as the new manager, to a brother-in-law's sheep station, Bundidgerry, near Narrandera, about 50 kilometres north-west of Wagga Wagga.[78] Morgan/Moran is *Robbery Under Arms*'s most feral bushranger, often likened to a black snake and presented as a merciless killer. But Ben Marston is also given few virtues in the novel. Unlike his wife, he isn't Irish; nor does he have any of Ned Kelly's insurrectionist hatred of the colonial state, despite being a transported convict. Although he is violent, he is politically subservient. 'Men like my father', Dick writes at one point, 'who have hated the breed [i.e. the English] and have suffered by them too, can't help having a curious liking and admiration for them. They'll follow them like dogs, fight for them, shed their blood and die for them'.[79] Ben Marston is especially loyal to Starlight, and is pleased when his daughter Aileen falls in love with the dashing bushranger. Starlight's history is generally unknown, but Dick identifies him as an 'Englishman [who] must have come young to the colony ... a gentleman to the tips of his delicate-looking fingers'.[80] When Starlight is shot and dying, he reminds the police inspector, Sir Ferdinand Morringer, that they had once shot pigeons together at Hurlingham, an exclusive sports club in London.

A reviewer in the Melbourne *Argus* thought that Starlight's aristocratic disposition made him an 'impossible' bushranger: 'I do not think there was ever such a man on the roads in Australia'.[81] At one point, the novel even casts Starlight (when he was *very* young?) as a seagoing adventurer. He is someone with the kind of experience we had seen with earlier global explorers like Dampier: 'He'd been all over the world—in the Islands and New Zealand; in America, and among the Malays and other strange people that we'd hardly ever heard of'.[82] Starlight also seems to have witnessed the brutalities of the slave trade. But he keeps a young Aboriginal companion, Warrigal, who is devoted to him but who Starlight beats and abuses in what is essentially a colonial master/slave relationship. Warrigal is a corruption of the Dharug word wuragal, meaning dingo or native dog. By the 1840s it began to be used pejoratively to mean *savage* or *wild*, or more commonly, as a synonym for Aboriginal people generally. *Robbery Under Arms* presents Warrigal as unwaveringly faithful to Starlight but also treacherous, finally betraying Dick Marston and the others to the police. These are the twinned racisms of the colonial adventure novel. He is killed soon afterwards by Dick's murderous—and literally deranged—father.

Apart from Warrigal, there are very few Aboriginal people in *Robbery Under Arms*. A settler nearby is married to 'a native girl who was born somewhere about the Hawkesbury, near Windsor'; there are a few Aboriginal police and trackers; and a 'small mob of blacks' gather to watch the bushrangers as they arrive at Berrima Gaol.[83] The word 'native' is now mostly claimed in the novel by non-Aboriginal characters, with the bushranger Moran, for example, described as 'a dark, thin, wiry-looking native chap'.[84] The bushrangers assume Aboriginal characteristics as well, and in doing so make Aboriginal people themselves seem redundant. Ben Marston could track in the bush 'as good as a blackfellow', for example, while Jim 'had a blackfellow's hearing'.[85] Aboriginal communities have been dispossessed from all the surrounding districts in this novel's historical setting. The bushrangers hide out at a place called Terrible Hollow, where there was once 'a tribe of blacks that inhabited the district'; a local Aboriginal woman—'Warrigal's mother, or aunt or something', Dick Marston casually remarks—is supposed to have revealed the location to 'the first white men' in the district.[86] There is an interesting scene in the novel where the bushrangers and Warrigal hunt and fish together in a river that runs through the hideout. Warrigal, Dick comments, would 'make nets out of cooramin bark, and put little weirs across the shallow places, so as we could go in and drive the fish in'.[87] Coolamon ('cooramin' in the passage) is an anglicised version of the Wiradjuri word guliman or gulaman, used to describe a bark container for carrying water, fruits and so on. This is a rare moment in *Robbery Under Arms*, where Boldrewood allows his Aboriginal character—whose family must have lived in the district—to demonstrate traditional cultural skills (in so far as Boldrewood understood them). The scene in fact presents an idealised but fleeting moment of castaway cohabitation. 'I feel as if I were living on an island', Aileen says when she comes to stay at the hideout later on. 'It's quite like playing at "Robinson Crusoe", only there's no sea ... It's a happy, peaceful life, too'.[88]

Boldrewood probably located Terrible Hollow in the Gwydir district in northern New South Wales. This is Gamilaroi, or Kamilaroi, Country.[89] It was also the site of a number of massacres of Aboriginal people just a few years before the novel properly begins: the Waterloo (or Slaughterhouse) Creek massacre in January 1838, where up to several hundred Gamilaroi people were killed; the Myall Creek massacre in June 1838, where at least twenty-eight Wirrayaraay people were killed by a vigilante group of settlers and convicts; and the Gwydir River massacre in August of the same year, where nine Gomeroi people were shot and killed by stockmen. (It may be worth asking: is Warrigal a Gomeroi man?) These massacres are precisely examples of what Fritzsche had called 'the "just passed" quality of a still half-remembered age'. But the novel doesn't see or acknowledge them. Even though it is set only a short time afterwards, it is also (to invoke the title of Fritzsche's book) 'stranded in the present'. *Robbery Under Arms* is an elegy for the 'last of the bushrangers', but not for the dispossession and killing of Aboriginal people. This must be at least in part because Boldrewood was himself involved in that dispossession—a term he then appropriated for himself. When in 1844 he established Squattlesea Mere—a property of around 50 000 acres—he declared that 'no white man could in any way disturb, harass, or dispossess me'.[90] He even imagined leading a 'splendid Robinson Crusoe kind of life' on his property, left to pursue the business of colonisation in his own way;[91] as if a squatter could somehow resemble a castaway, as Aileen imagines she is in Terrible Hollow.

But he found himself instead in the middle of the Eumeralla War, where Gunditjmara resistance fighters were struggling to protect their Country from a relentless wave of settler expansion. Under attack, Boldrewood speaks up for the squatters' right to 'behave in a quasi-legal manner' as Gunditjmara men engage 'in a guerrilla warfare' against them.[92] It is often noted that squatters 'closed ranks to protect each other' from legal scrutiny during this time as they aggressively defended their properties.[93] Native police arrive to assist with what Boldrewood euphemistically calls the Gunditjmara's 'chastisement' (rather like the term 'recruitment') and some of the key resistance fighters are killed. Later on, he writes derisively, 'the remnant of the tribe was gathered together and "civilised" at the missionary station of Lake Condah'.[94] But by the time we get to *Robbery Under Arms*, all these earlier historical moments are forgotten, or repressed. The squattocracy reigns supreme; Starlight respects the wealthiest squatters, and refuses to raid and steal from them. At the end of the novel, a group of squatters uses its political influence to secure Dick Marston's release from prison. Michael Howe, we remember, was killed wearing 'a dress made of kangaroo skins'—a politically radical figure linked to the 'wild' and viewed by colonial authorities as a deranged monster who must be executed. Marston, on the other hand, marries a squatter's daughter and becomes the manager of a property in Queensland (much like Boldrewood at Bundidgerry), absorbed into the most elite, powerful ranks of the colonial economy.

The Queensland novelist Rosa Praed is often praised for her portrayals of the New Woman and the Australian Girl, emerging proto-feminist character types that found their way into colonial fiction in the last decades of the nineteenth century.[95] In her novel *Outlaw and Lawmaker* (1893), the feisty Elsie Valliant is introduced as 'a model for some semi-allegoric Australian statue of Liberty'; on the other hand, she jokingly admits she would like to be 'carried off' by Moonlight, a bushranger active in the area.[96] Later on, she falls in love with him. Moonlight is actually Morres Blake in the novel: an aristocratic Irishman and 'Bohemian rebel',[97] who goes into politics, gets elected as a member of the Legislative Assembly and, remarkably, goes on to become colonial secretary. The first colonial secretary of Queensland was appointed in August 1859, soon after Queensland became a colony. Duties included responsibility for the police, and the native police.[98] So Blake/Moonlight is both the outlaw (robbing the colony) and the lawmaker (policing the colony) of the novel's title. Ned Kelly's fantasy at the end of the *Jerilderie Letter*, where the outlaw *is* the law, turns out to be true here.

The novel makes much of Blake/Moonlight's aristocratic nature, no doubt influenced by Boldrewood's Captain Starlight. Blake owns an extensive property called Barolin—his partner, the Fenian Dominic Trant, is the station manager—and is sometimes grandly introduced as 'Blake of Barolin'. Praed made up many of her place names: Queensland is 'Leichardt's Land', for example, and the novel's setting is 'the Luya district'. But Barolin was an actual place, located on the coastal plain around Bundaberg and named by the explorer Nugent Wade Brown, who thought it was an Aboriginal word meaning 'land of the kangaroo'.[99] In 1862 Barolin—a cattle station by this time—was leased by Arthur and Alfred Brown. Like Blake, Alfred Brown went on to become a Queensland politician: an

MLA in the early 1860s, and again from 1874 to 1882. This may well give us a general sense of the otherwise unspecified historical moment of *Outlaw and Lawmaker*—that is, the 1860s or 1870s—making it another bushranger novel about 'the "just passed" quality of a still half-remembered age'.

Typically, Praed gives no factual history of this place, and shifts the geography of Barolin around, taking it further inland. Elsie keeps asking how Barolin got its name, but no one answers her. Instead, Praed gives it a fabricated mythology. There is a 'Legend of Barolin', to do with a powerful Aboriginal warrior 'whom none of the other chiefs could stand'.[100] The chiefs kill the warrior, who is turned into a volcanic rock, hidden away behind a waterfall, 'which was called after him, Barolin'.[101] The novel then casts the site as a place that local Aboriginal people are afraid to visit: a squatter remarks, 'none of our Blacks will go near Barolin'.[102] It is also typical of Praed (and many other colonial novelists) to disparage Aboriginal spiritual beliefs by turning them into 'superstitions'.

But why was this Aboriginal warrior killed by other Aboriginal people? The novel certainly invests in a racist colonial ideology that saw Aboriginal people as *self*-extinguishing—an ideology often used to account for the role of the native police. But it may also be taking its revenge on a figure of Aboriginal resistance, who is then buried deep in the landscape and effectively cast out of colonial history. It is well known that Praed had her own traumatic experience of Aboriginal resistance as a child on her father's sheep station, Hawkwood, in the nearby Burnett district. On 27 October 1857 a number of Yiman people raided the Hornet Bank station along the

Dawson River, killing eight members of the Fraser family and three employees, including the family tutor. The attack may have been a response to the Fraser sons' sexual abuse of Yiman women.[103] Afterwards, the two surviving sons were involved in long-term, systematic reprisals; so was Praed's father, Thomas Lodge Murray-Prior, a squatter who was part of an infamous roving party or 'death squad' known as the Browns.[104] A Legislative Assembly inquiry into the Hornet Bank station killings was held in 1858, and one of the testimonies was in fact from Barolin's co-owner Alfred Brown, who had already been working in the district. Brown wanted a more efficient, ruthless native police force, to prevent any further Aboriginal resistance: something the inquiry agreed with. He was particularly suspicious of corroborees, which, he thought, gathered together 'blacks from all directions' to plan further attacks on settlers.[105]

Praed wrote about the Hornet Bank killings in the two autobiographies she published. In *Australian Life Black and White* (1885), she confesses, 'I have not ceased to dream that I am on an out-station besieged by Blacks.'[106] This is her never-ending trauma, extrapolated from her childhood. She repeats the same account of the Hornet Bank killings in more detail in *My Australian Girlhood* (1902), where her sense of settlers under attack in the district seems even more pervasive. In both books, she describes how—when she was about six years old—some young Aboriginal friends lead her to a secret corroboree, where she sees Yiman participants 'painted to represent skeletons, others in spiral stripes as though huge snakes were coiled round their bodies ....'[107] Praed gives us a colonial version of the primal scene here, where a young child sees something that should have remained hidden. Her overwrought use of the Gothic in her description of this corroboree intensifies her racist sense of the sheer Otherness of Yiman people, transforming them into the clichés of nightmare. But she also uses the scene to reproduce the paranoid colonial view that corroborees were indeed (as Alfred Brown thought) places where Aboriginal resistance to settler expansion could be gathered together and mobilised. 'Clearly', she writes, 'it is the rehearsal of a night attack upon some white man's station', adding guiltily: 'I have often thought that had I described to them [her parents] the ghastly performance I had witnessed, the Hornet Bank tragedy might have been averted'.[108]

It is generally agreed that Praed invented this account of the corroboree. It was Freud who had introduced the notion of a 'primal scene' (in this case, the child witnessing their parents having sex), suggesting that it might very well trigger 'retrospective phantasies of a later date'.[109] But Praed's recollections of the Fraser murders themselves were not even taken from her memory of actual events. They were taken instead from her father's written reminiscences later on; so there is already a deferral here, both to her own childhood and to Murray-Prior. As Patricia Clarke has noted, Praed '[wrote] herself into her father's accounts as a participant in events'.[110] Gordon Reid, who has looked closely at the Hornet Bank killings and subsequent reprisals, is even more scathing: 'Rosa Campbell Praed was responsible for more inaccurate statements about Hornet Bank than any other author'.[111]

Perhaps surprisingly, Praed revisited this (fabricated) corroboree all over again in a scene in her bushranger novel, where it is cast—some years later, in the novel's more recent historical setting—as a public (not hidden away or secret) performance for an invited white settler audience. It retains the racist grotesqueries of the autobiographical accounts, but now it is emptied of content: with the 'nightmare pattern' of body paint, for example, 'meaning nothing.'[112] The corroboree is completely dissociated from Hornet Bank or any other settler killings. Instead—perversely?—it acts as a kind of raw erotic stimulus for Blake/Moonlight and Elsie as they sit together and watch it. 'Blake was in wild spirits', the novel tells us; 'The excitement of the corroboree seemed to have infected him.'[113] When her dress touches Blake, Elsie is 'conscious almost of something electrical, highly charged in him'; soon afterwards, they go into the bush and kiss in a 'spirit of recklessness and passion.'[114] But their romance is not allowed to flourish. Later on, Elsie is kidnapped by Blake's partner, Trant, (not quite the abduction fantasy she had earlier entertained) and she is taken to the bushrangers' hideout by the Boralin waterfall, where, according to the 'legend' of the place, the Aboriginal warrior is buried. It turns out that Trant has betrayed Blake/Moonlight to the police. Blake arrives to rescue Elsie, and then, as the police close in, he throws himself over the waterfall to his death (much like Gypsey in Rowcroft's novel). So the self-extinction of a bushranger is folded into a 'legend' about the killing of an Aboriginal resistance fighter, yoking the two together. The novel then consigns these figures and all the things they stand for—Aboriginal resistance, colonial romance, wildness, adventure, etc—to a past that seemed momentous at the time but has now drawn to a close.

Outlaw and Lawmaker concludes rather abruptly, by sending Elsie away to Italy with her mother and then stretching its distance from the events that have only 'just passed': 'These things happened a good many years ago. This strange tragic episode was felt to be a blot on the history of Leichardt's Land ….'[115] The real 'blot' on Queensland's history, buried in the landscape of this novel, is to do with the killings at Hornet Bank and the long-term reprisals, involving her own father, that followed. These are then veiled with a 'legend' about Boralin and a bushranger romance that, for a moment, had seemed full of erotic possibility. But even these things are too close to those earlier events and must in turn (to recall Boxall) be 'purged away'—brought to life only to be unceremoniously shut down at the end and forgotten.

CHAPTER 5

The Speculations of Colonisation

EARLY COLONIAL EXPLORERS, as they ventured inland, aimed primarily to find land and water that would be suitable for farming and grazing stock, extending the range of settler occupation. This was the intention of the wealthy emigrant Gregory Blaxland, whose family were the owners of large estates in Newington, Kent. With William Wentworth, the surveyor William Lawson and a number of servants, Blaxland crossed Gulu-Mada/the Blue Mountains in May 1813. But was this journey an adventure? Blaxland published his *Journal of a Tour of Discovery Across the Blue Mountains* ten years later, in 1823. The word *tour* doesn't really imply much risk or danger, and although the men saw Aboriginal people, there were no close or violent encounters at this end of the frontier. A tour is not usually a detour, and the men were never lost or disoriented as they made their way to the edge of Wiradjuri (or Wiradyuri) Country. Blaxland got what he had hoped for, reporting that there was enough grass land there 'to support the stock of the colony for the next thirty years'.[1] *Tour* comes from the Old French *tourner*, to turn (round) or rotate, which suggests a circular journey, a circuit, that eventually leads you back to where you began. After four weeks in the mountains, the men returned to Warrane/Sydney and 'reached their homes, all in good health'.[2] A tour might seem harmless enough, but this one had devastating consequences for Aboriginal people. Blaxland and his company's route into the west led to the establishment of Bathurst on Wiradjuri Country, and an influx of settlers and farmers into the region. Acts of Aboriginal resistance (raids on outstations, etc) led to Governor Thomas Brisbane's 1824 declaration of martial law and increased levels of militarisation, and the bloody Bathurst War that saw at least a hundred Wiradjuri people killed.[3]

The figure of the state-sanctioned surveyor–explorer—like Lawson—helps to remind us that exploration and colonisation always went hand in hand. Thomas Livingstone Mitchell was appointed surveyor general of New South Wales in 1828. The colony's previous surveyor general, John Oxley, had tracked the course of the Galari/Lachlan and Wambuul/Macquarie rivers ten years earlier, hoping they would lead to 'the long sought for Australian sea', although he had 'nothing but conjecture for its basis'.[4] The notion of a yet-to-be-discovered river or sea in the Australian interior was in fact widely shared at the time. It provided the inspiration for the river-based explorations Mitchell himself undertook in the 1830s, and it informs most of the texts we'll examine in this chapter. Mitchell's exploration journals, *Three Expeditions into the Interior of Eastern Australia*, were published in 1838. We can note that the word *expedition* is a little different from *tour*, with clearer military connotations (from the Latin *expeditio*, meaning *campaign*) and a more determined sense of purpose. Even so, Mitchell's aim of finding an inland sea was little more than an act of faith and had drawn on a very dubious source. He had been listening to George 'The Barber' Clarke, an escaped convict and bushranger from the Liverpool Plains, who had cohabited with Kamilaroi people for nearly five years. In November 1831 the *Sydney Gazette* reported that Clarke had been arrested and taken to Bathurst, where he told the military commandant about a 'noble river'—known by the Kamilaroi, he claimed, as the Kindur—that ran all the way to Van Diemen Gulf, at the top of the Northern Territory. 'The man states that he traced the river to its mouth', the newspaper said,

> near to which he fell in with several tribes of natives, armed with bows and arrows, who informed him, by signs, that numerous boats occasionally came there ... [presumably] parties of Malays in prows, who came over to procure sandal wood and beech-le-mer [*sic*]—articles which form so valuable a part of their trade, particularly with China. In addition to these particulars, the narrator reports that he fell in with numbers of Hippopotamuses and Ourang Outangs—animals of whose existence in New Holland we have never before heard even a surmise.[5]

Mitchell seems to have completely believed Clarke's story, calling his first expedition 'Journey in Search of the Kindur, in 1831-32' and prefacing his journal with an account of what Clarke had claimed to have seen beyond the Liverpool Plains:

> He described the tribes inhabiting the banks of the 'Kindur' and gave the names of their chiefs. He said that he had first crossed vast plains named 'Balyran', and, on approaching the sea, he had seen a burning mountain named 'Courada'. He described, with great apparent accuracy, the courses of the known streams of the northern interior which united, as he stated, in the '*Nammoy*' [later, the Namoi], a river first mentioned by him; and, according to his testimony, Peel's River entered the 'Nammoy', by flowing westward from where Mr Oxley had crossed it.[6]

Oxley had named the Peel River after the British Tory politician (and, later, prime minister) Sir Robert Peel; it was, he wrote at the time, 'the largest interior river ... we had yet seen'.[7] But Clarke's story gave Mitchell a sense that there was something even greater out there, just beyond reach. The first expedition, he admits, 'originated in one of those fabulous tales ... respecting the interior country, still unexplored';[8] but he carried on, ever hopeful.

Mitchell invested in the romance of exploration, as if he was making a series of never-before-seen discoveries. 'There are few undertakings more attractive to the votaries of fame or lovers of adventure', he writes, 'than the exploration of unknown regions ... [we were] about to enter *Terra Incognita*'.[9] Like Cook, he named almost every place he saw on his travels, literally imprinting himself onto the landscape. His expeditions were entirely in the service of colonisation: 'we were to open a way for the many other beginnings of civilised man, and thus extend his dominion over some of the last holds of barbarism'.[10] The opposition between civilisation and barbarism became increasingly important to Mitchell as he ventured further west—although he also came to realise that Clarke's story was 'little else than pure invention'.[11]

Mitchell was not like Dampier: he admired many of the Wiradjuri people he met along the way. He also had an aesthetic appreciation of Aboriginal cultural practice, regarding a 'corrobory', for example, as 'the medium through which the delights of poetry are enjoyed' (in contrast to Rosa Praed's paranoia).[12] But when the party's botanist, Richard Cunningham, wandered off during the second expedition—a police inquiry later determined he was killed by Wiradjuri men—Mitchell's racism took on a darker tone. It intensified as he travelled west along the Baaka/Darling: 'The further we descended the river', he writes, 'the more implacably savage we found the blacks'.[13] Around this time, there was a 'collision' with some armed Aboriginal men, and one of Mitchell's party fired his gun several times. A Wiradjuri woman (carrying a child) was wounded and later died. Mitchell regretted the killing 'most bitterly' (we have seen colonial 'regret' a number of times in this book) but concluded that it was impossible 'to conciliate these people', the incident taking the explorers into 'a state of warfare'.[14]

When he returned to the Baaka/Darling on his third expedition in 1836, Mitchell was already primed for violent conflict. At one point, he becomes aware of (as he describes it) 'a vast body of blacks ... following our track, with prodigious shouting and war cries'.[15] A convict, Charles King, fires his gun and a large group of Aboriginal (Barkindji or Kureinji) people try to escape by swimming across the river. Other members of Mitchell's party also take the opportunity to load their guns and shoot. 'Much as I regretted the necessity for firing upon these savages', Mitchell writes, 'and little as the men might have been justifiable under other circumstances, for firing upon any body of men without orders, I could not blame them much on this occasion; for the result was the permanent deliverance of the party from imminent danger'.[16] Mitchell named the site of the massacre Mount Dispersion: another colonial euphemism. A memorial was erected there in 1963; in April 2020 the New South Wales government formally recognised it as a Declared Aboriginal Place.

Arriving back in Warrane/Sydney in November 1836, Mitchell found himself the subject of an official inquiry presided over by the New South Wales governor, Sir Richard Bourke. Some of the colonial newspapers were outraged by the killings. 'Is there ... any one thing adduced that could warrant thirty men firing on the natives', the *Sydney Gazette* asked, 'that could warrant their *reloading* ... to repeat the same act of destruction? Is there any thing that could justify a *second* volley, and a *third*, being discharged with the same awful effect?'[17] The *Australian*—the colony's second newspaper, with William Wentworth as one of its founders—noted that Mitchell, far from being in 'danger' by the river, carefully planned and executed an ambush: 'It is said that at least thirty [Aboriginal people] were slain; how many escaped with wounds does not appear'.[18] The inquiry itself was reported in John Dunmore Lang's weekly, the *Colonist*, which thought that Mitchell 'lightly presumed' the need to shoot and wrote about the killings in a 'spirit partaking more of exultation than regret'.[19] Mitchell himself wrote defensively to the inquiry, invoking Cunningham's murder, as well as the killing of Captain James Fraser on K'gari just a few months earlier; he also repeated his Manichean distinction between 'the civilised and the savage portion of our race'.[20] In the event, the inquiry recorded a 'Protest' over the massacre on the river. But it accepted Mitchell's report that seven (rather than the *Australian*'s estimation of thirty) Aboriginal people had been killed, agreed that the explorer's party must have been in a 'state of alarm', and shut down any further proceedings.[21]

One of the testimonies at the inquiry was from a Wiradjuri man from the Bathurst region known as John Piper, who had joined the third expedition as a guide and interpreter. Piper lent some support to Mitchell's sense of the unbridgeable difference between the 'civilised' and the 'savage', often talking disparagingly about '*Myalls*' or '*wild natives*' down river.[22] He helped to mediate with people from those remote communities, but he was also distant from them, and occasionally even violently hostile. We can imagine that Piper occupied a liminal position in the colony, a bit like Musquito, discussed in Chapter 4; but Mitchell came to heavily depend upon him for the expedition's success. Back in Warrane/Sydney, the artist and surveyor William Fernyhough (who had worked for Mitchell) produced a lithograph of Piper, with the Wiradjuri man dressed in a red coat Mitchell had given him and wearing a feathered hat that once belonged to Governor Darling. Piper wanted to return to his Country near Bathurst, so Mitchell gave him a gun and blankets, and a brass plate inscribed with the title *Conqueror of the Interior*:[23] which seems like both a colonising explorer's tribute to his faithful guide and a disturbing act of patronisation.

Some Wiradjuri women had also joined Mitchell's third expedition: Kitty ('a good strong woman'), as well as a young widow, Turandurey, and her four-year-old daughter, Ballandella. Mitchell much admired Turandurey's capacity as an intermediary. As she goes to greet an unfamiliar group of Wiradjuri people at one point, he comments:

> Our female guide ... stood now boldly forward, and addressed the strange tribe in a very animated and apparently eloquent manner; and when her countenance was thus lighted up, displaying fine teeth, and great earnestness of manner, I was delighted to perceive what soul the woman possessed, and could not but consider our party fortunate in having met with such an interpreter.[24]

Towards the end of the expedition, Mitchell thinks that Turandurey—this 'careful and affectionate ... mother'—is suddenly 'determined to entrust to me the care of [her daughter]'.[25] He gives a coloniser's reading of Turandurey's predicament, believing that she seeks a more secure future for Ballandella, with 'civilised men'.[26] Bringing the child back with him to Warrane/Sydney, he passed her on to a physician, Charles Nicholson (later, a powerful businessman and politician), when he left the colony and returned, temporarily, to Britain. For Mitchell, the removal of an Aboriginal child from her family is an opportunity for a racial (eugenic) 'experiment ... in developing hereafter, the mental energies of the Australian aborigines'; 'by the last accounts from Sydney', he proudly reports, 'I am informed, that she reads as well as any white child of the same age'.[27] But Ballandella, like her mother (and like Piper), maintained her liminal position in the colony. She had a child with a settler in 1846. A few years later, she married a Dharug or Darkinjung man, known in the colony as John Barber, and lived with 'a community of around twenty Aboriginal people' at Sackville Reach, on Dyarubbin/the Hawkesbury River.[28] In 1889 this site would become an Aboriginal reserve.

In her book *Meeting the Waylo* (2019), Tiffany Shellam looks at several examples of Aboriginal intermediaries who accompanied colonial explorers on their expeditions but who were usually treated as 'passive, faithful side-players' in what would typically be understood as 'heroic European efforts to map and make sense of a harsh and unforgiving environment'.[29] Perhaps the best-known Indigenous intermediary accompanying a European explorer was the extraordinary Tahitian navigator Tupaia, who sailed with Cook on the *Endeavour* (landing at Botany Bay in April 1770).[30] Shellam's first example of an Aboriginal intermediary is a Noongar man named Miago (she calls him Migeo), who had, among other things, travelled with the Swan River surveyor general, John Septimus Roe, to Menang Kort/King George Sound in 1835. Miago also accompanied John Lort Stokes on his 1838 expedition in Charles Darwin's old ship, the HMS *Beagle*, to the far northwest Australian coast. Recalling Piper's anxieties about so-called Myalls as he travelled inland from Warrane/Sydney, Miago was equally nervous about meeting remote northern communities.

These are the people Shellam calls the Waylo, a relatively uncommon term that seems to have appeared in print for the first time in an account given by two Noongar men to a Guildford settler in July 1834. It concerned some 'northern tribes (who appear to be indiscriminately referred to under the name of Waylo men, or Weel men)' who had discovered a shipwreck.[31] The diarist and landowner George Fletcher Moore—who was also an amateur linguist—had listed the word Welo in his *A Descriptive Vocabulary of the Language in Common Use Amongst the Aborigines of Western Australia* (1842), glossing it as: 'A name given to all people living to the north of them, by every tribe, be the latter situated where they may ….'[32] Stokes never actually used the word himself, but he noted that Miago 'evidently holds these north men in great dread.'[33] When Miago meets Jaburrara (Nyul Nyul) people to the north, near Ngariun Burr/Beagle Bay (named after the ship) in the Dampier Peninsula, he gives immediate expression to his liminal status: he 'threw open his shirt, and showed them his breast curiously scarred after their fashion … as a convincing evidence that he, though now the associate of the white man, belonged to the same country as themselves.'[34] Later, in early 1839, the explorer George Grey tried to recruit Miago and two other Noongar men in Boorloo/Perth as intermediaries for one of his own expeditions, but they didn't turn up. 'The length of the journey, and the danger of falling in with hostile tribes, had frightened them', Grey suggests (rightly or wrongly), 'and they, therefore, kept themselves aloof from us.'[35] Instead, he is joined by a Noongar man known as Kaiber, who we'll discuss below.

In England, Grey had written to Lord Glenelg, secretary of state for the colonies, proposing an expedition to the north of Derbal Yerrigan/Swan River, 'so as to intersect any considerable body of water, connecting it with the interior'.[36] The aim here—this time, without a bushranger's fabulous tales to guide them—was to find a river in Western Australia that matched the extensive water courses Mitchell had surveyed in the east. Glenelg approved the expedition, ordering Grey to 'familiarise the natives with the British name and character'.[37] The HMS *Beagle* set sail in July 1837, with Grey on board; he was twenty-five years old. At that time, the captain was John Wickham—who had earlier sailed with Darwin—with John Lort Stokes as first officer. At Cape Town, Grey hired a schooner, the *Lynher*, and sailed with a small crew (as well as sheep, goats and a number of dogs) to Hanover Bay on the north-west coast of Western Australia. The first expedition sees some of the crew come ashore 'beaming with delight and hope', with little sense, in Grey's words, of 'how soon our trials were to commence'.[38] This is an adventure that quickly deteriorates into a series of misadventures: the men are overwhelmed by the heat; some of the dogs die; the crew get sick from drinking brackish water; and when Grey tries desperately to get back to the *Lynher* for help, he realises he has 'attracted the notice of the natives'.[39] On board the schooner at last, he is grateful to have survived 'so many perils'.[40]

Grey was a very different kind of explorer from Mitchell: more emotionally entangled in his experiences, more candid about his fears and hardships, and more invested in using his journal to capture the excitement and drama of his adventures in narrative form. In his entry for 11 February 1838, he writes that around two hundred men, women and children—a 'fine race, tall and athletic'[41]—approach his camp and shout at the explorers to leave. Soon afterwards, one of the explorers runs towards Grey, 'breathless, and speechless with terror, and a native with his spear fixed in a throwing-stick in full pursuit of him; immediately a number of other natives burst upon my sight; each tree, each rock, seemed to give forth its black denizen, as if by enchantment'.[42] When a spear 'whistled past my head', Grey shoots an Aboriginal man in the arm. Another explorer tangles his gun in some cloth, while a third 'could do nothing but cry out, "Oh God! Sir, look at them; look at them!"'. This is a moment of sheer panic, the opposite of the measured confidence Mitchell showed when he orchestrated the 'dispersal' of Aboriginal people during his third expedition. When Grey does stand up to fire his gun, 'three spears struck me nearly at the same moment'.[43] Badly wounded, he manages to shoot an Aboriginal man but refuses to fire his gun a second time: this is again the opposite of Mitchell's party, who had reportedly reloaded their guns several times over.

When the attack is over, Grey and his party lose their way. He collapses in pain and sinks into a kind of romantic reverie, although he retains the alertness of a coloniser still desperate to preserve his life and mission:

> The sun shone out brightly, the dark forest was alive with birds and insects, – on such scenery I had loved to meditate when a boy, but now how changed I was; – wounded, fatigued, and wandering in an unknown

> land. In momentary expectation of being attacked, my finger was on the trigger, my gun ready to be raised, my eyes and ears busily engaged in detecting the slightest sounds, that I might defend a life which I at the moment believed was ebbing with my blood away.[44]

Grey's reverie then turns into a sort of elegy for himself, an ideological fantasy in which he imagines his own death and bestows a special status on himself as one of many explorers in a nation-to-come that will, he thinks, mourn his passing. Despite the misadventures, the failings, the immense pain of his wounds, he is able to maintain complete confidence in the fact of colonisation and its ultimate success:

> And in this way very many explorers yearly die ... A strange sun shines upon their lonely graves; the foot of the wild man yet roams over them; but let us hope when civilisation has spread so far, that their graves will be sacred spots, that the future settlers will sometimes shed a tear over the remains of the first explorer, and tell their children how much they are indebted to the enthusiasm, perseverance, and courage of him who lies buried there.[45]

Grey admired many of the Aboriginal people he met but had no vision for how they might exist in a colonised society. He did, however, develop an unusually close relationship with his Noongar intermediary, Kaiber. Kaiber accompanied Grey on his third expedition from Derbal Yerrigan/Swan River to Gutharraguda/Shark Bay in early 1839. Aboriginal intermediaries like Kaiber, Miago, Piper and Turandurey all left their Country and cohabited with expedition parties, often travelling great distances with them over a long period of time. This was *their* colonial adventure, which led to encounters (for example, with the 'north men', but also with the explorers themselves as well as settlers along the way) they may not otherwise have had. Recent commentaries have looked at Aboriginal 'mobility', and the capacity of precolonial Aboriginal people to travel widely and experience their own cross-cultural encounters.[46] But colonisation gave this a new inflection, with Aboriginal intermediaries developing relationships that could continue to influence their lives even after the expeditions were over (since colonisation, as we've noted before, doesn't go away).

Crossing the Gascoyne River, Grey sees some Yinggarda people who seem, once again, to be telling him to leave; but he is determined to make contact. Kaiber thinks these men are 'northern sorcerers' and is afraid of them. Grey directs him to speak to the Yinggarda and it appears that they, in turn, are 'dreadfully frightened' of the two men who have approached them.[47] The Yinggarda at first seem 'unintelligible' to Grey and Kaiber, but 'as they gained confidence', Grey realises (again, rightly or wrongly) that 'they spoke a dialect very closely resembling that of the natives to the north of the Swan River'.[48] Grey had learned Noongar language, and not long after this expedition he compiled *A Vocabulary of the Dialects of South Western Australia* (1840); it includes Way-lo (meaning 'the north') in its extensive list of Noongar words, although Grey didn't use the term in his expedition journals.[49] Grey and Kaiber talk to the

Yinggarda for a while and seem to understand what they say. When they finally leave—not to vacate the colony but (following the imperatives of colonisation) to go 'in search of new lands and adventures'[50]—Grey thinks that the dialects in the north are, to his surprise, more or less comprehensible to Noongar speakers. The Yinggarda are curious about the explorers in turn, asking them, 'Whence had we came? Where were we going to? Was the boat a dead tree?'[51] So this is an interesting encounter on the northern frontier: a non-violent moment of exchange and wonder that brings initially apprehensive people from different places (an explorer, a Noongar intermediary, the Yinggarda) into unexpected proximity with one another—resulting in a certain level of mutual interest and understanding.

After this encounter, the boats are wrecked in a storm, the explorers become increasingly weak and exhausted, and the expedition flounders: more misadventures. Grey finds himself relying on Kaiber's skills and expertise to find food and water, as they begin the long walk back to Boorloo/Perth. When the rest of the party are too depleted to continue, Kaiber urges Grey to leave them behind: 'to-morrow', he says, 'you and I will be two dead men if we walk not now'.[52] As they wander off to search for water, Grey thinks Kaiber has purposely led him astray. But Kaiber feels the expedition itself has led him away from his Country and wants to return home: 'He made a few protestations as to the folly of my conduct; [and] lamented most loudly that his mother, and the Dandalup (a river of his own land), were so far removed from him'.[53] There are significant moments of tension between Grey and Kaiber, but they also develop a touching intimacy that works to sustain them through the low points of the expedition. Sitting in the bush and 'lost in gloomy reveries and temporary unpopularity [with the exhausted men]', Grey writes that Kaiber 'lulled me with native songs, composed for the occasion'.[54] Later on, Grey transcribes the words of one of Kaiber's songs, which again expresses a longing to return home: 'Thither, mother oh, I return again, / Thither oh, I return again'.[55] The lyrics make Grey think of a lament sung by Miago's mother when her son had sailed with Stokes on the HMS *Beagle* earlier on:

> Whither does that lone ship wander,
> My young son I shall never see again.
> Whither does that lone ship wander.[56]

Grey includes a fascinating commentary on Aboriginal songs and poetry at the end of his journals, where (among other things) he elaborates a little further on this mother's lament for her absent son. He transcribes the song as follows:

> Ship bal win-jal bat-tar-dal gool-an-een,
> Ship bal win-jal bat-tar-dal gool-an-een,
> &c. &c. &c. &c.[57]

When Miago returns from the expedition to 'recount his adventures', a Noongar man composes another song, which Grey reproduces, or reconfigures, in the mode of a sea shanty:

> Kan-de maar-o, kan-de maar-a-lo,
> Tsail-o mar-ra, tsail-o mar-ra-lo.

&c. &c. &c. &c.
Unsteadily shifts the wind-o, unsteadily shifts the
wind-o,
The sails-o handle, the sails-o handle-ho.[58]

Clint Bracknell has suggested that Grey was the first colonial to appreciate a Noongar aesthetic in song and poetry, emphasising 'the importance of melody, presentation and delivery as affective qualities'.[59] Kaiber's song, and the songs sung by Miago's mother, offer some insight into the experience of a colonial adventure from an Aboriginal perspective—being away from home, 'wandering', sailing, wanting to return to Country—that would otherwise be difficult to access. Grey's journals have cultural value in this respect; they also offer moments of emotional candour—and vulnerability—that set his chronicles apart from Mitchell's.

Not everyone saw Grey in this way. Ernest Favenc was an explorer and popular novelist who in 1888 had visited the Gascoyne River, fifty years after Grey, helping to open up the region to development. As a 1908 obituary put it, 'No little debt of gratitude from the pastoral industry of Australia is due to Favenc, and to pioneers of like sterling calibre. He seldom engaged in wild-goose chases of purely speculative exploration'.[60] In his centennial study, *The History of Australian Exploration, from 1788 to 1888* (1888), Favenc spoke disparagingly of 'Grey's mishaps' and thought that the results of his expeditions 'were but meagre and of no very great importance'.[61] Dedicated to the New South Wales premier, Henry Parkes, Favenc's book was indeed a tribute to the successes of early colonial exploration, measured pragmatically in terms of the way it enabled colonisation to expand its range and generate wealth. But it was also a requiem for a series of earlier adventures that are now over: 'Since the hope of finding an inland sea, or main central range, vanished for ever', Favenc writes, 'the explorer cannot hope to discover anything much more exciting or interesting than country fitted for human habitation'.[62]

~

Was emigration to the colonies an adventure? It certainly meant leaving one's home, and heading somewhere new and distant: a journey that would always have involved some level of risk. But emigration also held up the promise of settlement: that is, of purchasing some property, building a house and making oneself at home all over again. In the early decades of the colonies, land (sometimes a great deal of land) was freely granted to settlers on behalf of the Crown. All this changed because of a man who was serving a sentence in Newgate Prison and had never actually visited Australia. Edward Gibbon Wakefield had been sent to Newgate for abducting a 15-year-old heiress from her Liverpool boarding school in March 1826 (the so-called 'Shrigley Abduction'). While behind bars, he wrote an extraordinary book in the first person—*A Letter from Sydney, the Principal Town of Australasia* (1829)—that imagines emigrating to New South Wales to take possession of a 20 000-acre property. The narrator buys 'herds and flocks, horses, ploughs, carpenters' tools and all sorts of implements of husbandry';

he rides the early wave of colonisation but is unable to find labourers willing to work for him.[63] Soon after he arrives, his servant leaves to take a property of his own, thanks to a grant of land 'near Hunter's River'.[64]

Wakefield's narrator quickly realises that the colonies are developing in a haphazard way: disorganised processes of land acquisition, unsustainable wages and not enough labourers to serve the rapidly growing economy. The solution Wakefield proposed was for government to shift from land grants to land sales at a 'sufficient price' (although he never specified what this was), and to use the money raised from sales to fund an assisted emigration scheme that would increase the labour force. This was a key part of what Wakefield called 'systematic colonisation'—although, as Jane Lydon has shown, it was also a pragmatic response to 'the demise of slavery', something Wakefield, as an anti-abolitionist, regretted.[65] Government-assisted emigration began in the early 1830s and significantly increased the number of free settlers in the colonies. Land was divided up into blocks to be sold off to new arrivals, and cities such as Tarndanya/Adelaide were planned in the same way, laid out as a set of straight 'grids' over the colonial landscape. Wakefield had no interest in Aboriginal people; he saw these blocks as 'waste land', unoccupied sites that were simply waiting for settlers to take possession. We can note that this is the way commercial land dealers, real estate agents, auctioneers and so on routinely continue to give expression to *terra nullius*. As Geoff Park has commented, Wakefield's scheme essentially 'liberat[ed] future inhabitants from any sense of place in which native or indigenous things matter'.[66]

Towards the end of the 1830s, the real estate investor Thomas Walker travelled with a small group of men from Warrane/Sydney down to Nerm/Port Phillip, to look at land sales and purchase property (including a significant part of Naarm/Melbourne's CBD). It was a journey he chronicled in *A Month in the Bush of Australia* (1838); a narrative full of 'tedious and unnecessary' details that, he writes, would nevertheless be useful to 'those who have intentions of Emigrating'.[67] Walker's book is a sort of anti-adventure—he calls it an 'extensive tour'—which sees the travellers follow closely, and safely, in the footsteps of Mitchell's third expedition. It is a purposeful journey, and they never detour, wander off or get lost; as Walker puts it, they 'never diverged to either side of their route'.[68] Although he occasionally meets Aboriginal people along the way, his journey is essentially a tribute to the new settlements of colonisation: a list of 'estates', farms and houses that he visits, the 'improvements' made to properties, and the resources settlers can access to help them to prosper. In September 1838 the Sydney *Herald* published a letter addressed to Walker from someone signed 'Viator' (from the Latin *viātor*, meaning 'traveller'), under the heading 'Emigration'. 'The settler is no longer an adventurer', the letter astutely suggests, 'but a speculator, who estimates the expenses and probable advantages of his undertaking ... Other measures will be necessary to remove what may be called, impediments to occupation'.[69] This writer recognises a shift in the logic of the colonial adventure narrative, as colonisation establishes itself and extends its range and influence. The adventurer has devolved into a speculator: after Wakefield, what brings emigrants out to the colony—and what makes surveyor–explorers go in search of inland rivers—is now much more explicitly to do with capital, investment, property and home-making. But Viator's letter also gives euphemistic, ominous expression to the dark side of such speculation. This isn't quite Wakefield's sense of blocks of property for sale as *terra nullius*. But while it does give veiled acknowledgement to the prior habitation of Aboriginal people, it also makes clear that (as 'impediments to occupation') colonisation's success depends upon their complete and total dispossession.

Thomas McCombie's novel *Arabin; or, the Adventures of a Colonist in New South Wales* (1845) turns the shifting ground Viator's letter describes into a narrative that sees its young emigrant protagonist become a successful property speculator; it also includes a frank assessment of the worth of Wakefield's land sale reforms. McCombie himself had emigrated from Scotland when he was twenty-two, arriving in Melbourne in 1841. He was a grazier for a while and developed a successful political career. From 1844 to 1851 he was editor and part owner of the *Port Phillip Gazette*, the region's second newspaper (after John Fawkner's short-lived *Melbourne Advertiser*). In McCombie's novel, Godfrey Arabin is 'a young man of enthusiastic temperament', who is 'fond of fictitious and speculative literature', especially the works of Sir Walter Scott.[70] Drawing on an inheritance from his father, Arabin studies medicine at Edinburgh. But he squanders his money—'he would rush heedlessly into the most absurd speculations', the novel tells us—and soon realises that he is heading for ruin.[71] He decides to emigrate to the colonies to begin his life all over again.

Arabin's early experiences as a country doctor in what would later become western Victoria see him continue his restless life, romantically feeling as if he could 'wander the country with an erratic tribe of black men, and see one spot to-day, another to-morrow ….'[72] But he meets two graziers who make him rethink his options. The first is Jack Willis, a dandy and a 'wild' profligate, who has also squandered all his money.[73] As the novel goes on, Willis becomes increasingly deranged, and quickly descends into lunacy; Arabin is repulsed by him. The second is a married settler called Butler. 'Give me a comfortable home, plenty of money, and allow me to live comfortably', he says to Arabin.[74] The novel pauses at one point to think about settlers as a character type. Settlers, it suggests, are emigrants who have given up their 'wandering' spirit. They are not adventurers; like Butler, they prefer homely comforts and 'steady habits'.[75] In Chapter 1, we mentioned the critic Franco Moretti's view of Daniel Defoe's Robinson Crusoe as a prototype of the acquisitional, industrious bourgeois. A characteristic of Crusoe's bourgeois tastes is that he values comfort above everything else as he goes about making a home on his island, where 'everyday necessities' are 'made pleasant'.[76] In McCombie's novel, settlers are the colonies' bourgeoisie, aiming to be comfortable (like Crusoe), productive, industrious and aspirational (also like Crusoe). Arabin finds himself increasingly drawn to this ideological position. Influenced by Butler and in love with his sister-in-law, he gets another small inheritance and buys some property, becoming not only a settler, but a squatter: 'stock was the best speculation', he realises.[77]

McCombie's novel wants its squatters/settlers to speculate, but it also wants to minimise the risks. 'There has been a spirit of reckless speculation abroad in the Australian Colonies', it tells us, 'which has brought many of the apparently wealthy to insolvency. The majority of them will do no good in the future ....'[78] An economic depression had led the judge Sir William Burton—who had famously presided over the second trial of the Myall Creek massacre in 1838, sentencing seven settlers to death—to draft the *Insolvent Law of New South Wales* (1842). This was designed 'to enable bankrupts to return to productive enterprise'—that is, to keep the colonial economy going.[79] Even so, in *Arabin* it is better to 'pursue an even, steady course' than to overspeculate and slide into bankruptcy.[80] It helps if land is cheap and squatters could have security of tenure. This is McCombie's criticism of Wakefield: that his reforms actually *increased* the chances of insolvency, by inflating the cost of land, and reducing the opportunity for investment and future development. 'What is there to encourage capitalists to come here?' he writes, interrupting his novel again to criticise the 'fireside economist' from Newgate Prison; 'Let the land be reduced to 5s. and prosperity will once more dawn on our Australian settlers ...'[81] McCombie was a colonial libertarian, who thought Wakefield's form of systematic colonisation was 'too prohibitive'. He didn't like government interference, generally speaking (unless it helped the squatters), and thought the assisted emigration fund did little more than drain capital from hard-working landowners.[82] His novel is a tribute to the *laissez-faire* colonial capitalist who is aspirational but not extravagant. Yet when Arabin is eventually successful, married and settled, the novel has nowhere else to go.

It brings the various speculations of the 'emigration adventure' to a close by recognising that what follows—settlement itself—can only seem 'tedious' by comparison.[83]

Early on, the novel's trajectory towards a condition of total settlement across the colonies is momentarily unsettled by a 'tale of horror', involving the killing of five Aboriginal women a few years earlier at a place called Mount Misery, not far from Butler's property. 'Some young men came up the river on a frolic', Butler explains to Arabin; 'they had brandy in their boat, of which they drank large quantities. They became testy, and quarrelled. Then the smoke of the encampment of blacks at this Mount was perceived.'[84] After the killings, the men hide the bodies and leave. But the next morning, 'they recovered their senses, and of course remorse began to prey on their minds; they had dyed their hands in human blood, and troubled consequences would not allow them to rest in peace'.[85] All except one of the men flee the colonies for England, India and South America, Butler says; 'there was no sentence recorded against any of the party', but the settler who remained behind 'ended his days in a mad-house', while the others each died either by suicide or 'violent death'.[86] Aboriginal people have minor, subordinate roles in McCombie's novel. But, at one point, an Aboriginal man named Dermott tells Willis that he doesn't steal sheep precisely because he knows about the extent of settler reprisals and settler killings. 'Plenty kill blackfellow', he says; 'One black fellow kill sheep, white fellow plenty take him, and him plenty killed.'[87] Butler's account of settlers killing Aboriginal women isn't explicitly to do with settler reprisals, but it is interesting to note that while no legal judgement holds the settlers accountable, the novel delivers them up to its own form of moral retribution.[88]

In an appendix to *Arabin*, 'An Essay on the Aborigines of Australia', McCombie mentions the actual massacre his novel's 'tale of horror' was based on. This is a generally racist essay but—in contrast to Wakefield's idea of the colonies as 'waste land'—it at least recognises that Aboriginal people 'possess a certain acknowledged territory'.[89] Typically sceptical of government initiatives, McCombie thinks the Protectorate Establishment in the Nerm/Port Phillip District—set up by Lord Glenelg in 1838, in an attempt to provide some 'humanitarian' support to Aboriginal people—was 'a total failure'.[90] He then mentions the killing of an Aboriginal woman he calls 'Conger':

> A murder was committed at Muston's Creek, we believe on the 23rd February, 1842. A native woman ... was barbarously murdered in a tea-tree scrub. Three settlers, Richard Gumeas Hill, John Beswick, and Joseph Betts, were indicted for the murder, and tried before Mr Justice Jeffcot, at Port Phillip, on the 31st July 1843. It was evident a murder had been committed, and several even thought that the prisoners were the murderers; but opinion was divided, and the evidence being contradictory, the men were found 'Not Guilty'. So far well, – the men were tried before a jury, and they had a chance, and it would have been cruel to deprive them of their chance. The Protectors thought otherwise: they spoke of the jury in terms which would disgust my readers ...[91]

This is a squatter's version of what came to be known as the Spring Creek massacre, where four Gunditjmara women and a child were killed while sleeping among some tea-trees near Muston Creek. McCombie reduces the fatalities to one Gunditjmara woman. There were not three but six or seven, possibly eight, settlers involved in the killings: Hill, Beswick, Betts and others, including the licensee of the nearby Spring Creek station, Robert Whitehead. The massacre had nothing to do with drunkenness. As Michael F Christie has noted, it was a 'premeditated' act probably organised by Whitehead; a paramilitary settler attack during the later years of the Eumeralla War (taking place a couple of years before Boldrewood arrived in the district: see Chapter 4).[92]

Ian D Clark has looked closely at the events leading up to these killings, in his book *Scars in the Landscape: A Register of Massacre Sites in Western Victoria* (1995), and lists the names of the four murdered women: Connyer, Natgoncher, Wooigouing and Wonigoniber. (The name of the murdered child is not known.) Two Gunditjmara survivors reported the reprisal killings to the assistant protector and rewards were offered for more information. Whitehead and another murderer fled the colony as a consequence (although Whitehead returned later on), but Hill, Beswick and Betts were indeed arrested, and brought to trial in Melbourne's Supreme Court in July and August 1843, with Redmond Barry conducting the prosecution. The lawyer representing the three accused men told the court: 'gentlemen, there is no person entitled to so much protection as the settler, for it is from him all our wealth is derived; our commerce flourishes through his industry'.[93] At the end of the trial, the judge began to speak, but the foreman presented him with notice that the jury—'comprised mostly of squatters', some of whom 'were themselves tainted by their own participation in other massacres'[94]—had already made up their minds. They pronounced the three men Not Guilty.[95] Interestingly—remembering what had happened to the murderers in *Arabin*'s 'tale of horror'—an assistant protector 'commented that two of the prisoners died shortly after; he was relieved that "there is certainly retributive justice even to the blacks"'.[96]

McCombie's novel was reprinted in 1850 without its 'tale of horror'; effectively deleting this particular massacre from his tribute to the 'adventure' of emigration and settlement. This was the same year he published his infamous *Essays in Colonisation*, hardening his racism by totally conforming to Viator's chilling notion that all 'impediments to occupation' must be removed. 'Colonisation is undertaken for the advantage of the migrating people', McCombie insisted, 'and the aboriginal races stand in the way of the immigrants'.[97] A few pages later, he replaces his earlier recognition of Aboriginal claims to 'a certain acknowledged territory' with a stark expression of Australia as *terra nullius*, nothing more than blocks of 'waste land' waiting to be discovered, bought and developed by eager new arrivals. Adventure carves out the initial path, and the dream of what McCombie calls 'extensive colonisation' inevitably follows. His account of all this is worth comparing with Swift's description of how colonisation works, presented in Chapter 1:

> A few adventurers from it [England] arrive in an unoccupied country, and go forth into the wilderness

> as the pioneers of civilisation—the number gradually increase, the settlers as a matter of course, require towns and villages to supply them with necessaries, and thus shipping and mercantile interests arise—agriculture is deemed profitable and followed by numbers, and the country is rapidly developed. By-and-bye, we have population increasing, the country lined with rail-roads, and the streams and rivers ploughed with steamboats, until the "terra incognita" of Australia is changed into a great and populous nation.[98]

~

The *Eclectic Review*, an influential British Nonconformist journal, reviewed Thomas Mitchell's *Three Expeditions into the Interior of Eastern Australia* in February 1839, reprimanding the explorer for his 'deplorable acts against the Aborigines of the interior', and for overvaluing 'our rights in the soil of Australia' while 'underrating ... the rights and character of the true owners of that soil'.[99] Alongside Mitchell, the journal also reviewed a fantasy exploration adventure along the lines of Swift's *Gulliver's Travels*. The book's title, *Account of an Expedition to the Interior of New Holland* (1837), seemed to mimic (or anticipate, since it was published a year earlier) Mitchell's work. Lady Mary Fox was credited as the book's editor; the reviewer calls her 'the ingenious author of this new Utopia'.[100] Fox was the daughter of the Duke of Clarence (later, William IV) and his mistress Dorothea Jordan; she never visited Australia, although she had lived in Canada for a while with her husband, Charles Richard Fox, before becoming the housekeeper at Windsor Castle. There is general agreement, however, that the actual author of this work was Richard Whately, the political economist and (at the time) archbishop of Dublin. We mentioned Whately in Chapter 2, in the context of convict transportation as a self-defeating 'method of colonisation'. In a letter in late 1837, another political economist, Harriet Martineau, noted that 'Whately is the author of the "Utopia", edited by Lady Mary Fox. He wishes this to be known, though he could not, as archbishop, publish it himself'.[101] On the other hand, reprinted editions of this work in 1849 and 1860—under the new title, *The Southlanders*—suggest it was 'compiled by more than one person', perhaps including Fox herself.[102]

Account of an Expedition to the Interior of New Holland presents the incredible journal of a fictional explorer, Hopkins Sibthorpe. With the help of a settler, two naval officers and a servant, Sibthorpe builds a large canoe, and the party set off together from Bathurst in 1835, rowing along the length of a large river until they come to a 'great expanse of water, so extensive that, in pursuing their adventurous course nearly in the same direction, they were, for the greater part of one day, out of sight of land'.[103] So this is another inland sea fantasy: it has this in common with the bushranger George Clarke's fabulous tales that had inspired Mitchell's first expedition. The explorers see pigs and cattle, and fertile, cultivated land, and soon they realise they are in the midst of a huge European settlement that, it turns out, has been living in the Australian interior for around three hundred years. The inhabitants—'three or four million' of them—were originally refugees from Europe. Fleeing the 'various tumults' of the Reformation, they had boarded ships and sailed southward, 'induced by some glowing descriptions they had heard ... to seek for the long-famed southern continent, the "Terra Australis Incognita".'[104] Shipwrecked along the coast, they encounter some hostile Aboriginal communities ('savages'), but these are kept at a distance: much as they were in a similar southland fantasy, *The Travels of Hildebrand Bowman*, discussed in Chapter 1. There are very few violent conflicts on this particular frontier. Instead, the Europeans manage to build their settlements and live peacefully with some 'native allies', encountering almost no resistance. As the novel puts it, 'The European and aboriginal races became in time completely blended together', all equally 'admissible to the rights of citizenship.'[105] This is the novel's Utopia—or, as it calls it, 'Eutopia.' The idea seems noble enough; but the fantasy turns out to be one of total colonisation (a bit like McCombie's 'extensive colonisation'), with these shipwrecked Europeans bypassing dispossession altogether, in order to claim a right of prior occupation and full governance of their territories. In a nod to Wakefield, each person rents a 'suitable allotment' from the state, developing it in whatever way they wish.[106] The novel is a Robinson Crusoe fantasy escalated to its maximum capacity, with Sibthorpe's adventure taking him by boat deep into the interior of New Holland, only to find that he is already at home, that settlers are everywhere and settlement is literally all over the place. There is nothing in this fantasy that colonisation hasn't already reached.

In Chapter 1, we mentioned several early imaginary voyages that charted the surprising discovery of 'ideal Commonwealths' that had long ago migrated to a remote region of the Antipodes: like *Hildebrand Bowman*. Fox's *Southlanders* belongs to this genre, sometimes known as 'lost world' or 'lost race' romance—and, later on, as Lemurian romance. Sumathi Ramaswamy has talked about the 'obscure and humble birth' of the term 'Lemurian', which first appeared in an article published in 1864 by the zoologist Philip Lutley Sclater, as a way of accounting for the seemingly impossible migration of people from one continent to another at some distant historical moment.[107] Later on, the eugenicist Ernst Haeckel took up the term in his book *The History of Creation* (1876), drawing on Sclater to posit the existence of a continent called Lemuria as 'the probable cradle of the human race' and the source of migration routes to the rest of the world.[108] Haeckel's view of racial hierarchies—with white people at the top of the ladder—was part of a vogue in evolutionary thinking at the time that also manifested itself in speculative explorer fiction: notably, H Rider Haggard's best-selling novel *She: A History of Adventure* (1887), which saw a group of men follow mysterious instructions that take them to the interior of east Africa, where they encounter 'an evolutionarily degenerate African civilisation and its immortal queen isolated in a remote mountain valley and lost to historical time'.[109]

In colonial Australia, the Lemurian novel flourished in the 1890s, with explorers heading inland to encounter racially or culturally unfamiliar civilisations that would often similarly be cast as 'evolutionarily degenerate'.[110] Some of these novels also imagined, belatedly now, the discovery of an inland sea. A striking Haggardian example is the Adelaide-born W Carlton Dawe's *The Golden Lake* (1891), which sees two young adventurers, with an Aboriginal (possibly Wiradjuri) intermediary named Jimmy, from 'somewhere on the Murrumbidgee River,'[111] go off into the Western Australian interior. Here, they find an inland lake, and hidden piles of gold and rubies, as well as a sacred 'Great White City' inhabited by the Mandanyah people: canoe-building warriors, who practise human sacrifice, ruled over by a ferocious king, Kalua. The novel unleashes its racism at every opportunity, with the adventurers loading their guns and shooting as many 'hostile' Aboriginal people as they can, without registering any regret at all. Eventually, when they get to the Great White City, they kill the king himself. The novel is also a colonial captivity narrative, with a white woman, Ada—who had been living with the Mandanyah—rescued by the adventurers and taken to safety. *The Golden Lake* is pure destruction and desecration, an indication of how articulations of racism in the colonies intensified and became increasingly grotesque as the nineteenth century wore on. 'The white man never yields', one of the blustering adventurers says, as he loads up his gun yet again:[112] this is the sheer banality of late colonial adventure fiction, which can no longer be bothered to understand or tolerate any world other than its own. In the event, a volcano erupts, and the Mandanyah are buried, along with all the gold and precious stones. The adventurers make their way back to Boorloo/Perth, with nothing much except a few rubies, and Ada, now a fetish object for the narrator. Jimmy at least returns to 'his beloved Murrumbidgee', although he is put to work on a squatter's station.[113]

We'll close this book with a discussion of another racist Lemurian novel that is at the same time a delirious tribute to colonial adventure fiction's *fin de siècle* dream of what total colonisation could deliver—and also, like Mitchell and Fox, imagines the existence of an inland sea. John David Hennessey emigrated from England to Australia in 1875, when he was twenty-seven. A Methodist minister with an interest in journalism, he moved to Warrane/Sydney to establish the *Australian Christian World*, floating it on the stock exchange for £1 per share as part of a bid to make the Christian media central to the business of colonial nation building.[114] In the 1890s Hennessey turned his attention to agriculture and farming techniques, launching the monthly *Australian Field* in 1894, and writing a popular series of newspaper articles under the name 'The New Chum Farmer': that is, a farmer newly arrived in the colonies (even though he had been there for some time). A couple of years later, he published a Lemurian adventure novel, *An Australian Bush Track* (1896), which took the idea of speculative fiction literally, by introducing a protagonist, the 'new chum' Bright Hartley, who is a speculator, an investor in property and the stock markets, now living in Meeanjin/Brisbane. Brimming with an emigrant's confidence and optimism, he tells two of his wealthy friends that 'some of the biggest strokes of luck, and queerest adventures too, which have befallen men in any part of Australia have happened to the newly arrived ....'[115]

Hartley shows his companions a letter apparently written by Captain James Cook himself, dated 16 May 1770, when the *Endeavour* was anchored off Cape Moreton, Quandamooka Country. The letter wants to 'place on record a true and circumstantial account of a singular and well-nigh incredible occurrence' that was too fabulous to include in his official journal of the voyage.[116] A 'large native vessel' seems to approach the *Endeavour* and an apparently 'hostile' Aboriginal man throws a boomerang at the ship. The crew fire at him, although Cook (like Mitchell later on) insists that he is 'anxious to maintain friendly relations with the natives'.[117] Under attack, the vessel suddenly disappears. Disturbed by the experience, Cook examines some mysterious symbols engraved on the boomerang and decides to take it back to England to be deciphered. In fact, Cook was indeed in Moreton Bay at this time, writing in his voyage journal that he saw 'about twenty' Quandamooka people on the beach. To his surprise, they completely ignore the presence of his ship: 'not one of them was observed to stop and look towards us, but they trudged along, to all appearance, without the least emotion either of curiosity or surprise, though it is impossible they should not have seen the ship by a casual glance as they walked along the shore'.[118] Cook himself thought the ship must have surely seemed to the Quandamooka a 'little less stupendous and unaccountable than a floating mountain with all its woods would have been to us'.[119] He imagines that seeing his ship would have been an awesome hallucinatory experience for local Aboriginal people; Hennessey's novel inverts this conceit by giving the hallucinatory experience to Cook. The boomerang turns out to have directions to an inland sea, and a golden city with white gates. Hartley is incredibly excited by what he has discovered and quickly organises an expedition with his two friends: 'He was smitten with a malady only known in new lands—the desire to exploit a new and unknown territory and, if possible, discover undreamt-of sources of wealth'.[120]

The novel then shifts its attention to a young woman, Dorna Stoneham, who is searching for her missing sister, Marjorie. Dorna somehow makes her way towards the same inland sea, and finds her sister married and settled in a large homestead on a 'wonderful bit of country' alongside what looks like an ocean. This is a bit like Fox's *Southlanders*, where settlers miraculously inhabit inland Australia long before explorers finally get there. Hennessey calls the district 'Beulah Land', a reference to John Bunyan's famous Christian dream-allegory, *The Pilgrim's Progress* (1678), where the Land of Beulah is a fertile and delightful place of 'orchards and vineyards' that leads directly to the gates of Heaven.[121] It turns out this Lemurian adventure is driven by nothing less than an evangelical mission to exploit the vast resources it imagines are awaiting explorers—and settlers—in the Australian interior. Hartley arrives with his friends, and they find a track that leads to a 'taboo' place they defiantly enter: 'men will go into queer spots, won't they,' he says, 'when there's the prospect of adventure and *gold*?'[122]

This is the all-too-familiar colonial logic of a mining company: that no place is sacred when it comes to the pursuit of precious resources. (Think, for example, of Rio Tinto's destruction in May 2020 of a sacred cave at Juukan Gorge in Karijini/the Hamersley Range that had indicated 46 000 years of continual occupation by Aboriginal people.) A group of strangers approaches the explorers, 'dressed in a quaint kind of tunic, richly embroidered'; this is the novel's lost race, 'a remnant of a great nation which came [to Queensland] from some part of the mainland of Asia'.[123] The tribe willingly hands over huge amounts of gold and diamonds, leading Hartley to imagine how easy it would be simply to take possession of the entire desert 'on a mining lease'.[124] 'I am going to float a great gold and diamond company ... when we get back from this trip', he says, providing his friends with a detailed breakdown of investment, cost, profits, etc.[125] As the explorers leave with their treasure, a devastating thunderstorm brings a deluge of rain, flooding the region. Marjorie and Dorna rescue them on a yacht that flies a Union Jack; they repel a series of attacks by Aboriginal people, who have otherwise been absent from the novel (Dorna shoots a young man in the wrist as he is about to strike Hartley); and, finally, they arrive safely back at Marjorie's well-stocked frontier homestead.

It is worth remembering that the largest mining company in Australia (and the world), BHP, the Broken Hill Proprietary Company, was established and floated on the stock exchange in 1885, ten years before Hennessey's novel was published. In Queensland, where the novel is set, gold was discovered at Charters Towers (Gudjal Country) at the end of 1871—coincidentally, during a fierce thunderstorm. By 1890 Charters Towers was Queensland's second-largest town, connected by a railway and known locally as The World because it seemed entirely self-sufficient, as if it had everything it could possibly need. The Charters Towers goldfields were immensely productive, so much so that the town opened its own Stock Exchange (now a heritage-listed building). At the end of Hennessey's novel, Hartley is the CEO of the Central Australian Desert Tunnel Gold Mining Scheme, with plans for a railway, an 'inviting' prospectus for future shareholders, and an expectation that 'the company might pay dividends to the tune of a million per annum'.[126] This is the novel's unrestrained fantasy—feeding off the success of actual mining ventures like Charters Towers—where total colonisation begins and ends with the accumulation of tremendous wealth.

An Australian Bush Track has no interest in its lost race beyond an expectation they will cheerfully hand over piles of gold to colonial speculators. Unlike so many of the earlier adventure narratives we have looked at, it doesn't even have any ethnographic curiosity about Aboriginal people, who are seen simply as 'impediments to occupation' that must be left behind. This is colonial adventure stripped back to its barest elements, playing out an almost exhausted formula that even its own characters know only too well. 'You two fellows', Hartley says to his companions, 'came to Australia simply because you were at a loose end. After roaming and shooting and yachting, and all the rest of it, over half the world, you profess to find nothing new under the sun ....'[127] Adventurers have indeed become speculators, investors and company agents at this point, although no doubt they always were. If we recall the opening comments in Chapter 1 on the establishment of the Dutch East India Company, we'll remember this was the first company in the world to make equity shares publicly available on a stock exchange. By the time of Hennessey's novel, adventure narratives seem to have emptied themselves of any imperative other than the personal enrichment of their protagonists. At the same time, the possibility of any kind of self-transformation *during* the adventure is minimal, since there is now 'nothing new under the sun'. Even so, the speculator's insistence on the right to take their companies almost anywhere and extract whatever they want continues, as much today as ever before.

Endnotes

Introduction

1 Georg Simmel, 'The Adventurer', in Donald N Levine, ed., *Georg Simmel: On Individuality and Social Forms* (Chicago: University of Chicago Press, 1971), p. 188.

2 Ibid., p. 188.

3 Georg Simmel, 'The Stranger', ibid., p. 143; our italics.

4 See Cedric J Robinson, *Black Marxism* (Chapel Hill: University of North Carolina Press, 2000), pp. 9–27. Robinson's book was first published in 1983.

5 Trevor Burnard and John Garrigus, *The Plantation Machine: Atlantic Capitalism in French Saint-Domingue and British Jamaica* (Philadelphia: University of Pennsylvania Press, 2016), p. 3.

6 Kris Manjapra, *Colonialism in Global Perspective* (Cambridge: Cambridge University Press, 2020), pp. 7–8.

7 Cited in Ann Curthoys and Jessie Mitchell, *Taking Liberty: Indigenous Rights and Settler Self-Government in Colonial Australia, 1830-1890* (Cambridge: Cambridge University Press, 2018), p. 371.

8 Amanda Nettelbeck, 'From Humanitarianism to Humane Governance: Aboriginal Slavery and White Australia', in Joy Damousi, Trevor Burnard and Alan Lester, eds, *Humanitarianism, Empire and Transnationalism, 1760-1995: Selective Humanity in the Anglophone World* (Manchester: Manchester University Press, 2022), p. 185.

9 David Meredith and Deborah Oxley, 'The Convict Economy', in Simon Ville and Glenn Withers, eds, *The Cambridge Economic*

History of Australia (Cambridge: Cambridge University Press, 2014), p. 100.

10 See Emma Christopher, 'From the Caribbean to Queensland: Re-examining Australia's "Blackbirding" Past and its Roots in the Global Slave Trade', *Conversation*, 4 June 2021.

11 Tracey Banivanua-Mar, *Violence and Colonial Dialogue: The Australian-Pacific Indentured Labour Trade* (Honolulu: University of Hawai'i Press, 2007), p. 1.

12 George Palmer, *Kidnapping in the South Seas; Being a Narrative of a Three Months' Cruise of H.M. Ship Rosario* (Edinburgh: Edmonston and Douglas, 1871), p. 108.

13 George Palmer, letter to the Crown Solicitor, 16 August 1869, *New South Wales. Notes and Proceedings of the Legislative Assembly During the Session of 1871-2*, Vol. 1 (Sydney: Thomas Richards, Government Printer, 1872), p. 506.

14 Anon., 'The Daphne Case', *Queenslander*, 9 October 1869, p. 9.

15 Cited in A Grove Day, *Louis Becke* (Melbourne: Hill of Content, 1967), p. 148.

16 Louis Becke, 'The Wreck of the Leonora: A Memory of "Bully" Hayes', *Ridan the Devil and Other Stories* (Philadelphia: JB Lippincott Company, 1899), p. 281. For a good discussion of Becke's many versions and representaions of Hayes in his fiction, see Chrystopher John Spicer, 'The Granite and the Rainbow: Towards a New Biography of Louis Becke', *Journal of the Association for the Study of Australian Literature,* 21:2 (2021).

17 Louis Becke, 'Collier: The "Blackbirder"', *Pacific Tales* (Philadelphia: JB Lippincott Company, 1896), p. 166.

18 Robin DG Kelley, 'Foreword', in *Black Marxism*, p. xiv.

Chapter 1

1 See, for example, Lodewijk Petram, *The World's First Stock Exchange*, trans. Lynne Richards (New York: Columbia University Press, 2014).
2 James Backhouse Walker, ed., *Abel Janszoon Tasman: His Life and Voyages* (Hobart: William Grahame Jr., 1896), p. iv.
3 See Nicholas Thomas, *Cook: The Extraordinary Voyages of Captain James Cook* (New York: Walker & Company, 2003).
4 William Howitt, *The History of Discovery in Australia, Tasmania, and New Zealand,* Vol. 1 (London: Longman, Green, Longman, Roberts, and Green, 1865), p. 110.
5 Bernard Smith, *European Vision and the South Pacific* (1959; Melbourne: The Miegunyah Press, 2022), p. 11.
6 John Byron, *The Narrative of the Honourable John Byron* (London: S Baker and G Leigh, 1768), p. 257.
7 John Byron, *A Voyage Round the World, in His Majesty's Ship The* Dolphin (London: J Newberry and F Newberry, 1868), 'Preface', n.p.
8 Ibid., p. 182.
9 Nicholas Thomas and Oliver Berghof, eds, *A Voyage Round the World: George Forster*, Vol. 1 (Honolulu: University of Hawai'I Press, 2000), p. xxvi.
10 Ibid., p. xxvii.
11 William Dampier, *A New Voyage Round the World* (London: James Knapton, 1699: fourth edition), p. 352.
12 Ibid., p. 465.
13 Shino Konishi, *The Aboriginal Male in the Enlightenment World* (London: Taylor & Francis, 2015), p. 54.
14 Ibid., p. 466.
15 Ibid., p. 466.

16 Richard Bodek and Joseph Kelly, eds, *Maroons and the Marooned: Runaways and Castaways in the Americas* (Jackson, US: University Press of Mississippi, 2020), p. 1.

17 John Davies, trans., *The History of the Caribby-Islands* (London: Thomas Dring and John Starkey, 1666), p. 202.

18 William Dampier, *A New Voyage*, p. 481.

19 Ibid., p. 487.

20 Ibid., p. 519.

21 Cited in Geraldine Barnes, 'Curiosity, Wonder, and William Dampier's Painted Prince', *Journal for Early Modern Cultural Studies*, 6:1 (Spring–Summer 2006), p. 33.

22 Philip Edwards, *The Story of the Voyage: Sea-Narratives in Eighteenth-Century England* (Cambridge: Cambridge University Press, 1994), p. 20.

23 Adrian Mitchell, *Dampier's Monkey* (Adelaide: Wakefield Press, 2010), pp. 26, 164.

24 Barbara Fuchs, *Knowing Fictions: Picaresque Reading in the Early Modern Hispanic World* (Philadelphia: University of Pennsylvania Press, 2021), pp. 1–2.

25 Ibid., p. 1.

26 William Dampier, 'Preface', *A Voyage to New Holland* (London: James Knapton, 1703), n.p.

27 Ibid., n.p.

28 Ibid., n.p.

29 Ibid., n.p.

30 Ibid., p. 123.

31 Ibid., p. 146.

32 Ross Gibson, *The Diminishing Paradise: Changing Literary Perceptions of Australia* (Sydney: Angus & Robertson, 1984), pp. 10–11.

33 John Howell, *The Life and Adventures of Alexander Selkirk* (Edinburgh: Oliver & Boyd, 1829), p. 64.

34 Ibid., p. 94.

35 Daniel Defoe, *The Life and Strange Surprizing Adventures of Robinson Crusoe* (London: W Taylor, 1719), n.p.

36 See Franco Moretti, *The Bourgeois: Between History and Literature* (London and New York: Verso, 2013), pp. 25–35.

37 Defoe, *Life and Adventures*, p. 42.

38 Daniel Carey, 'Reading Contrapuntally: *Robinson Crusoe*, Slavery, and Postcolonial Theory', in Daniel Carey and Lynn Festa, eds, *The Postcolonial Enlightenment: Eighteenth-Century Colonialism and Postcolonial Theory* (Oxford: Oxford University Press, 2009), p. 115.

39 James Joyce, 'Daniel Defoe', trans. Joseph Prescott, *Buffalo Studies*, 1 (1964), p. 25.

40 Jonathan Swift, *Travels into Several Remote Nations of the World, By Captain Lemuel Gulliver*, Vol. 2 (London: Benjamin Motte, 1726), pp. 318, 320.

41 Ibid., p. 321.

42 Ibid., p. 322.

43 See, for example, Glyndwr Williams, *The Great South Sea: English Voyages and Encounters, 1570–1750* (New Haven: Yale University Press, 1997), p. 210.

44 Swift, *Travels*, Vol. 2, pp. 339–40.

45 Ibid., pp. 346–47.

46 Ibid., p. 347. Declan Kibberd writes of this passage: 'There is something almost hysterical about Gulliver's desperate defence of the British nation: if he were a slightly more complex thinker, the sentence might be taken as sarcasm on his part, but it is safer to attribute that to Swift': Declan Kibberd, *Irish Classics* (Cambridge, MA: Harvard University Press, 2001), p. 90.

47 Henry Neville, *The Isle of Pines; or a Late Discovery of a Fourth Island, in Terra Australia Incognita* (London: T Cadell, 1668), p. 12.

48 Gabriel de Foigny, *A New Discovery of Terra Incognita Australia, or the Southern World, by James Sadeur, a French-man* (London: John Dunton, 1693), pp. 3, 10.

49 Ulrich Beck, 'The Cosmopolitan Perspective: Sociology in the Second Age of Modernity', in Steven Vertovec and Robin Cohen, eds, *Conceiving Cosmopolitanism: Theory, Context, and Practice* (Oxford: Oxford University Press, 2002), p. 83.

50 Simon Tyssot de Patot, *The Travels and Adventures of James Massey* (London: John Watts, 1733), p. 9.

51 Ibid., p. 11.

52 Ibid., pp. 226–27.

53 Ibid., pp. 317–18.

54 John Hawkesworth, 'Preface', *An Account of the Voyages Undertaken by the Order of His Present Majesty for Making Discoveries in the Southern Hemisphere*, Vol. 1 (London: W Strahan and T Cadell, 1773), n.p.

55 Ibid., n.p.

56 On the authorship of this work, see Lance Bertelsen, 'Introduction', *The Travels of Hildebrand Bowman* (Peterborough, Ontario: Broadview Press, 2017), p. 35: 'The author of Hildebrand Bowman has not been definitively identified. The two most likely candidates are John Elliot ... a midshipman on the *Resolution* during Cook's second voyage, and Robert Home ... an English painter of Scottish ancestry'.

57 Anon., *The Travels of Hildebrand Bowman* (London: W Strahan and T Cadell, 1778), n.p.

58 Ibid., pp. 8–9.

59 George Forster, *A Voyage Round the World*, Vol. II (London: B White, J Robson, P Elmsly and G Robinson, 1777), p. 458.
60 For a useful discussion of cannibalism and the Grass Cove killings, see Anne Salmond, *The Trial of the Cannibal Dog* (New Haven: Yale University Press, 2003) pp. 223–31.
61 *Hildebrand Bowman*, p. 122.
62 Ibid., p. 380.
63 Leslie Bodi, 'Introduction' to Therese Huber, *Adventures on a Journey to New Holland*, trans. Rodney Livingstone (Melbourne: Lansdowne Press, 1966), p. 5.
64 *Adventures on a Journey*, pp. 36–7.
65 Ibid., p. 49.
66 Ibid., p. 346.
67 Ibid., p. 49.
68 Ibid., pp. 93, 115.
69 Lisa O'Connell, 'Before *Frankenstein*: Therese Huber and the Antipodean Emergence of Political Fiction', *Postcolonial Studies*, 23:3 (2020), p. 353.
70 *Adventures on a Journey*, p. 121.

Chapter 2

1 John Dunmore Lang, *Transportation and Colonisation* (London: AJ Valpy, 1837), p. 42.
2 Richard Whately, *Remarks on Transportation, and on a Recent Defence of the System* (London: B Fellowes, 1834), p. 164.
3 Lang, *Transportation*, p. 31.
4 Anon., 'Fugitives', *Sydney Gazette and New South Wales Advertiser*, 5 March 1803, p. 3.
5 Anon., 'Sydney', *Sydney Gazette,* 19 June 1806, p. 1.
6 Ibid., p. 1.

7 Charles Dickens, *Great Expectations* (London: Chapman and Hall, 1862), p. 2. On the chronology of the novel, see Mary Edminson, 'The Date of the Action in *Great Expectations*', *Nineteenth-Century Fiction*, 13 (June 1958), pp. 22–35.

8 Michael Flynn, 'Second Fleet', *The Dictionary of Sydney*, 2016.

9 Cited in Cassandra Pybus, *Black Founders: The Unknown Story of Australia's First Black Settlers* (Sydney: UNSW Press, 2006), p. 113.

10 See, for example, Emma Christopher, '"The Slave Trade is Merciful Compared to [This]": Slave Traders, Convict Transportation, and the Abolitionists', in Emma Christopher, Cassandra Pybus and Marcus Rediker, eds, *Many Middle Passages: Forced Migration and the Making of the Modern World* (Berkeley: University of California Press, 2007), p. 112–13.

11 FM Bladen, ed., *Historical Records of New South Wales – Phillip, 1783-1792*, Vol. 1, Part 2 (Sydney: Charles Potter, Government Printer, 1892), p. 53.

12 Jane Lydon, *Anti-Slavery and Australia: No Slavery in a Free Land?* (London: Routledge, 2021), p. 71.

13 Watkin Tench, *A Complete Account of the Settlement at Port Jackson, in New South Wales* (London: G Nicol and J Sewell, 1793), p. 137.

14 Ibid., p. 141.

15 Grace Karskens gives a sceptical reading of Tench's account in '"This spirit of emigration": the nature and meanings of escape in early New South Wales', *Journal of Australian Colonial History*, 7 (2005), pp. 19–22. She suggests instead that these convicts used the idea of travelling to China as a kind of strategy or ruse to make the authorities regard them as 'deluded' and punish them less severely upon their return.

16 See FM Bladen, ed., *Historical Records of New South Wales – Hunter, 1796-1799*, Vol. 3 (Sydney: Charles Potter, Government Printer, 1895), p. 360.
17 (George Barrington?), *History of New South Wales, including Botany Bay, Port Jackson, Parramatta, Sydney, and All its Dependencies* (London: M Jones, 1802), pp. 100, 218, 231.
18 Anon., 'Fatal Excursion', *Sydney Gazette*, 26 June 1803, p. 4.
19 Benjamin Mountford, *Britain, China, and Colonial Australia* (Oxford: Oxford University Press, 2016), pp. 17–19.
20 Tim Causer, ed., *Memorandoms by James Martin: An Astonishing Escape from Early New South Wales* (London: UCL Press, 2017), p. 11.
21 Ibid., p. 22.
22 *Complete Account of the Settlement*, p. 108.
23 Ibid., p. 109n.
24 Tim Causer, 'Introduction', in Tim Causer, Margot Finn and Philip Schofield, eds, *Jeremy Bentham and Australia: Convicts, Utility and Empire* (London: UCL Press, 2022), p. 4. No one seems to know how Bentham got hold of Martin's manuscript.
25 *Memorandoms*, p. 87.
26 Ibid., pp. 146–47.
27 Paul Carter, *The Road to Botany Bay: An Exploration of Landscape and History* (Minneapolis: University of Minnesota Press, 2010), p. 301.
28 '"This spirit of emigration"', pp. 7, 34.
29 Ian Duffield, 'Cutting Out and Taking Liberties: Australia's Convict Pirates, 1790–1829', *International Review of Social History*, 58 (December 2013), p. 197.
30 Ibid., p. 227.
31 James Porter, *Autobiography of convict James Porter, written on Norfolk Island 1840-1844*, State Library of New South Wales (DLMSQ 604), p. 6.

32 Ibid., p. 21.

33 James Porter, 'A Narrative of the Sufferings and Adventures of Certain of the Ten Convicts, Who Piratically Seized the Brig "Frederick" at Macquarie Harbour, in Van Diemen's Land ...', *The Hobart Town Almanack and Van Diemen's Land Annual* (Hobart Town: William Gore Elliston, 1838), pp. 6, 7.

34 See RD Keynes, *Charles Darwin's Beagle Diary* (Cambridge: Cambridge University Press, 1988), p. 292.

35 *Autobiography of convict James Porter*, p. 45.

36 Alexander Maconochie, *Australiana: Thoughts on Convict Management and Other Subjects Connected with the Australian Penal Colonies* (London: John W Parker, 1839), pp. 2, 21.

37 *Autobiography of convict James Porter*, p. 62.

38 Anon., *The Life and Surprising Adventures of Blue-Eyed Patty, The Valiant Female Soldier* (c.1790), p. 6, State Library of New South Wales collection.

39 [Sophia Edwards], *Surprising Misfortunes of Sophia Johnson. Written by Herself* (Chester: J Williams, 1838), p. 3, National Library of Australia collection.

40 Ibid., p. 6.

41 Richard Cobbold, *The History and Extraordinary Adventures of Margaret Catchpole, A Suffolk Girl* (New York: D Appleton & Co., 1846), p. 56.

42 Ibid., p. 91.

43 Ibid., pp. 145, 146.

44 Ibid., pp. 148, 167.

45 John Nicol, *The Life and Adventures of John Nicol, Mariner* (Edinburgh: Blackwood, 1822), p. 4.

46 Ibid., p. 71, 95.

47 Ibid., p. 190.

48 Ibid., p. 119.

49 Ibid., p. 139.

50 Ibid., p. 211.

51 James Francis Hogan, ed., *The Convict King, Being the Life and Adventures of Jorgen Jorgenson* (London: Ward & Downey, 1891), pp. 68, 69.

52 Ibid., p. 147.

53 Ibid., p. 37.

54 Jorgen Jorgenson, 'A Shred of Autobiography', *Hobart Town Almanack and Van Diemen's Annual* (Hobart Town: James Ross, 1835), p. 115.

55 *The Convict King*, p. 188.

56 Ibid., p. 29.

57 Jorgen Jorgenson, 'Original Correspondence', *Hobart Town Advertiser*, 31 June 1840, p. 2.

58 E Morris Miller, *Australia's First Two Novels: Origins and Backgrounds* (Hobart: Tasmanian Historical Research Association, 1958), p. 6.

59 Henry Savery, *Quintus Servinton. A Tale Founded Upon Incidents of Real Occurrence*, Vol. 1 (Hobart Town: Henry Melville, 1830), p. 221.

60 Ibid., Vol. 3, p. 334.

61 (James Tucker), *The Adventures of Ralph Rashleigh: A Penal Exile in Australia, 1825-1844* (Hawthorn, Victoria: Lloyd O'Neill, 1970), p. 17.

62 Ibid., p. 72.

63 Ibid., p. 214.

64 Ibid., p. 245.

65 Christine Wright, *Wellington's Men in Australia: Peninsular War Veterans and the Making of Empire c. 1820–1840* (London: Palgrave, 2011), p. 173.

66 *The Adventures of Ralph Rashleigh*, pp. 246, 247.

67 See, for example, Laurie Hergenhan, *Unnatural Lives: Studies in Australian Fiction about the Convicts, from James Tucker to Patrick White* (St Lucia: University of Queensland Press, 1983), p. 16. Paul Giles makes the same point again much later on in 'The Global Invention of the Australian Novel', in David Carter, ed., *The Cambridge History of the Australian Novel* (Cambridge: Cambridge University Press, 2023), p. 17.

68 On earlier translations of de Sade's work into English, including *Justine*, around the time of *Ralph Rashleigh*, see Will McMorran, 'The Marquis de Sade in English, 1800–1850', *Modern Language Review*, 112:3 (July 2017), pp. 549–66.

69 Frances Ferguson, *Pornography, the Theory* (Chicago: University of Chicago Press, 2004), p. 61.

70 *The Adventures of Ralph Rashleigh*, p. 290.

71 Ibid., p. 297.

72 Ibid., p. 315.

73 Ibid., p. 316.

74 Ibid., p. 338.

75 Ibid., p. 349.

76 Ibid., p. 349.

77 Lurline Stuart, ed., *Marcus Clarke, His Natural Life* (St Lucia: University of Queensland Press, 2001), p. xlix.

78 Marcus Clarke, *For the Term of His Natural Life* (London: Richard Bentley, 1886), pp. 91, 106.

79 Ibid., p. 107.

80 Ibid., p. 216.

81 Ibid., p. 260.

82 Ibid., p. 152.

83 Ibid., p. 360.

84 Stuart Macintyre, *A Concise History of Australia* (Cambridge: Cambridge University Press, 2004), p. 69.

85 *For the Term*, pp. 390, 391.

86 Ibid., p. 409.

87 Ibid., pp. 462–63.

88 John Shillinglaw, 'Review', *Herald*, 9 May 1874, p. 3.

Chapter 3

1 Angela Woollacott, *Gender and Empire* (Basingstoke: Palgrave Macmillan, 2006), p. 38.

2 See Penelope Edmonds and Amanda Nettelbeck, eds, *Intimacies of Violence in the Settler Colony* (Palgrave, 2018), p. 7.

3 David Collins, *An Account of the English Colony in New South Wales* (London: T Cadell and W Davies, 1798), p. 407.

4 Grace Karskens, *People of the River: Lost Worlds of Early Australia* (Sydney: Allen & Unwin, 2020), p. 121.

5 Ibid., p. 121.

6 Ibid., p. 122.

7 *An Account of the English Colony*, p. 424.

8 Ibid., p. 424.

9 John Maynard and Victoria K Haskins, *Living with the Locals: Early Europeans' Experience of Indigenous Life* (Canberra: National Library of Australia, 2016), p. 14.

10 *An Account of the English Colony*, p. 457.

11 *People of the River*, pp. 368–69.

12 William Buckley, *Reminiscences of James* [sic] *Buckley Who Lived for Thirty Years Among the Wallawarro or Watourong Tribes at Geelong Port Phillip, communicated by him to George Langhorne* (1837), p. 3. State Library of Victoria's Manuscripts Collection.

13 Ibid., p. 4.

14 Ibid., p. 4.

15 The relative was George Frederick Belcher, a local pastoralist and trader and, for a couple of years in the 1870s, mayor of Geelong.

16 *Reminiscences*, p. 5

17 Ibid., p. 5.

18 Ibid., pp. 11–12.

19 'William Buckley', *Age*, 29 July 1911, p. 4.

20 See, for example, Rebe Taylor, *Unearthed: The Aboriginal Tasmanians of Kangaroo Island* (Adelaide: Wakefield Press, 2008), p. 56: 'Morgan wrote the book as if he were Buckley …'.

21 John Morgan, *The Life and Adventures of William Buckley* (Hobart: Archibald MacDougall, 1852), p. 17.

22 Ibid., pp. 17–18.

23 Ibid., p. 25.

24 Ibid., p. 30.

25 Ibid., p. 99.

26 James Dawson, *Australian Aborigines: The Languages and Customs of Several Tribes of Aborigines in the Western District of Victoria, Australia* (Melbourne: George Robertson, 1881), p. 110.

27 Ibid., p. 110.

28 Ibid., p. 111.

29 *The Life and Adventures*, p. 110.

30 Ibid., p. 114.

31 Ibid., p. 120.

32 Ibid., p. 125.

33 The island had been known to settler Australians as Fraser Island for many years. It was officially given its Butchulla name, K'gari, on 7 June 2023.

34 Kay Schaffer, *In the Wake of First Contact: The Eliza Fraser Stories* (Cambridge: Cambridge University Press, 1995), p. 89.

35 See, for example, Kate Darian-Smith et al., *Captured Lives: Australian Captivity Narratives* (London: Sir Robert Menzies Centre for Australian Studies, 1992); Schaffer's *In the Wake of First Contact*; and Kate Darian-Smith, '"Rescuing" Barbara Thompson and other white women: captivity narratives on Australian frontiers', in Kate Darian-Smith, Liz Gunner and Sarah Nuttall, eds, *Text, Theory, Space : Land, Literature, and History in South Africa and Australia* (London: Routledge, 1996).

36 Larissa Behrendt, *Finding Eliza: Power and Colonial Storytelling* (St Lucia: University of Queensland Press, 2016), p. 184.

37 Christopher Castiglia, *Bound and Determined: Captivity, Culture-Crossing, and White Womanhood from Mary Rowlandson to Patty Hearst* (Chicago: University of Chicago Press, 1996), p. 4.

38 See, for example, John Curtis, *Shipwreck of the Stirling Castle* (London: George Virtue, 1838), p. 128.

39 Eliza Fraser, *Narrative of the Capture, Sufferings, and Miraculous Escape of Mrs Eliza Fraser* (New York: Charles S Webb, 1837), p. 7.

40 Ibid., p. 7.

41 Kate Fullagar, *The Savage Visit: New World People and Popular Imperial Culture in Britain, 1710–1795* (Berkeley, CA: University of California Press, 2012), p. 6.

42 *Narrative of the Capture*, p. 19.

43 *Shipwreck of the Stirling Castle*, p. 75.

44 Ibid., p. 62.

45 Harry Youlden, 'Shipwreck in Australia', *The Knickerbocker*, Vol. XLI, No. 4 (April 1853), p. 295.

46 Ibid., p. 291.

47 Robert Gibbings, *John Graham, Convict, 1824* (1937; London: John Dent, 1956), p. 63.

48 Olga Miller, 'K-gari, Mrs Fraser and Butchulla Oral Tradition', in Ian J McNiven, Lynette Russell and Kay Schaffer, eds, *Constructions of Colonialism: Perspectives on Eliza Fraser's Shipwreck* (London and New York: Leicester University Press, 1998), p. 35. Miller notes that Mrs Fraser had complained to the rescue party that Davis/Durumboi had raped her, an accusation he denied, p. 35.

49 JS Ryan, 'The Several Fates of Eliza Fraser', *Journal of the Royal Historical Society of Queensland*, 11: 4 (1981), pp. 97–99.

50 (Constance Campbell Petrie), *Tom Petrie's Reminiscences of Early Queensland* (Brisbane: Watson, Ferguson & Co., 1904), pp. 262–63.

51 John MacGillivray, *Narrative of the Voyage of H.M.S. Rattlesnake*, Vol. 1 (London: T & W Boone, 1852), p. 301.

52 Ibid., p. 305.

53 Ibid., p. 305.

54 Victoria K. Haskins, 'Women's Work and Cross-Cultural Relationships on Two Female Frontiers: Eliza Fraser and Barbara Thompson in Colonial Queensland, 1836-1849', in Penelope Edmonds and Amanda Nettelbeck, eds, *Intimacies of Violence in the Settler Colony* (Basingstoke: Palgrave, 2018), p. 139.

55 *Narrative of the Voyage*, p. 306.

56 OW Brierly, 'Journals of H.M.S. Rattlesnake', in David R Moore, *Islanders and Aborigines at Cape York: An Ethnographic Reconstruction Based on the 1848-1850* Rattlesnake *Journals of O.W. Brierly and Information He Obtained from Barbara Thompson* (Canberra; Australian Institute of Aboriginal Studies, 1979), pp. 76–77.

57 Ibid., p. 92.

58 *Living with the Locals*, p. 152.

59 'Information obtained from Barbara Thompson, 16 October – 12 November 1849', in *Islanders and Aborigines*, p. 144.

60 *Narrative of the Voyage*, p. 308.

61 Ibid., p. 308.

62 Emma Dortins, *The Lives of Stories: Three Aboriginal-settler Friendships* (Canberra: ANU Press, 2018), p. 14.

63 Morrill's phrase is reproduced in David Malouf's novel *Remembering Babylon* (London: Vintage, 1993), when a character, Gemmy, emerges from the bush and says to a boy and his dog, 'Do not shoot ... I am a B-b-british object!' p. 3. Malouf's treatment of Gemmy gave rise to a number of debates during this time about the way the contemporary Australian novel understood colonisation.

64 *Living with the Locals*, p. 182.

65 Cited in Ross Gibson, *Seven Versions of an Australian Badland* (St Lucia: University of Queensland Press, 2002), p. 89.

66 Stephanie Anderson, *Pelletier: The Forgotten Castaway of Cape York* (Melbourne: Melbourne Books, 2012), p. 27.

67 William Jackman, *The Australian Captive; or, An Authentic Narrative of Fifteen Years in the Life of William Jackman* (Auburn, USA: Derby and Miller, 1853), p. 72. In *Leviathan* (1651), the English philosopher Thomas Hobbes famously declared that people in a 'state of nature' existed 'in that condition which is called Warre; and such a warre, as is of every man, against every man': *Leviathan* (Oxford: Oxford University Press, 1901), p. 96.

68 *The Australian Captive*, pp. 100, 142.

69 Ibid., p. 217.

70 Ibid., p. 281.

71 Ibid., p. vi.

72 Ibid., p. v.

73 Ibid., pp. v–vi.

74 Ibid., p. iv.

75 DW Carnegie, *Grien on Rougemont; or the Story of a Modern Robinson Crusoe* (London: Edward Lloyd, Ltd. [*Daily Chronicle*], 1898), p. 10.

76 (William G Fitzgerald), 'Introduction', *Wide World Magazine*, Vol. 1, No. 1 (May 1898), p. 3.

77 (William G Fitzgerald), 'The Adventures of Louis de Rougemont', *Wide World Magazine*, Vol. 1, No. 5 (September 1898), p. 451.

78 William G Fitzgerald, 'Preface', *The Adventures of Louis de Rougemont, As Told By Himself* (London: George Newnes, Ltd., 1899), p. x.

79 Ibid., pp. 194, 199.

80 Anon., 'A Magnificent Hoax', *Leader*, 29 October 1898, p. 21.

81 For a local account of the *Daily Chronicle*'s London 'trial', see, for example, 'The Rougemont Romance', *Daily Telegraph*, 27 October 1898, p. 3.

82 Cited in Anon., 'De Rougemont's "Wide World" Stories: The Two Tallest', *Brisbane Courier*, 12 November 1898, p. 2.

83 *Grien on Rougemont*, p. 19.

84 Ibid., p. 19.

85 See, for example, 'A Modern Munchausen', *Leader*, 8 October 1898, p. 21: 'He is a Munchausen, Monte Cristo and Robinson Crusoe rolled into one'.

86 Amanda Nettelbeck and Robert Foster, *In the Name of the Law: William Willshire and the Policing of the Australian Frontier* (Adelaide: Wakefield Press, 2007), p. 2.

87 For an account of events behind this particular killing, see Sam D Gill, *Storytracking: Texts, Stories & Histories in Central Australia* (Oxford: Oxford University Press, 1998), pp. 66–68.

88 With Walter Baldwin Spencer, Gillen later worked closely with Arrernte people; their influential ethnographic work, *The*

Northern Tribes of Central Australia, would be published in 1904.

89 WH Willshire, *A Thrilling Tale of Real Life in the Wilds of Australia* (Adelaide: Frearson and Brother, 1895), p. 11.

90 Ibid., pp. 12, 24.

91 Ibid., p. 45.

92 Ibid., p. 62.

Chapter 4

1 See Mollie Gillen, Yvonne Browning and Michael Flynn, *The Founders of Australia: A Biographical Dictionary of the First Fleet* (Australia: Library of Australian History, 1989) and Ian Duffield, 'Martin Beck and Afro-Blacks in Colonial Australia', *Journal of Australian Studies*, 9:16 (1985), pp. 3–20.

2 'Martin Beck', pp. 15–16.

3 *An Account of the English Colony*, p. 70.

4 Ibid., p. 72.

5 Ibid., pp. 71–72.

6 Ibid., p. 444.

7 Stephen Gapps calls him 'John Wimbo', a 'gamekeeper and settler [who] had spent much time in the bush and with Aboriginal people and was known for "harbouring them and feeding them in his house"': see Gapps, *The Sydney Wars* (Sydney: NewSouth Publishing, 2018), p. 139.

8 Ibid., p. 457.

9 Alexander Harris, *Martin Beck; or, The Story of an Australian Settler* (London: G Routledge and Co., 1852), pp. 16–17.

10 'Martin Beck', p. 15; and see, for example, Cassandra Pybus, *Black Founders*, p. 3.

11 Anon., 'Parramatta', *Sydney Gazette and New South Wales Advertiser*, 17 February 1805, p. 2.

12 Anon., 'Sydney Gazette', *Sydney Gazette and New South Wales Advertiser*, 2 March 1806, p. 2.

13 The author of *Michael Howe* is often identified as Thomas Wells, an emancipated convict, landowner and clerk: see, for example, George Mackaness's Introduction to his edition of *Michael Howe: The Last & Worst of the Bushrangers of Van Diemen's Land* (Exile Bay: ETT Imprint, 2021), pp. 5–6.

14 *Michael Howe*, p. 6. Mansong was the subject of William Earle's novel *Obi; or, The History of Three-Fingered Jack* (1800).

15 James Boyce, *Van Diemen's Land* (Melbourne: Black Inc., 2018), p. 76.

16 Ibid., p. 76.

17 *Michael Howe*, p. 12.

18 Anon., 'Hobart Town', *Hobart Town Gazette*, 12 April 1817, p. 2.

19 *Michael Howe*, p. 30.

20 Ibid., p. 33.

21 Ibid., p. 31.

22 Ibid., p. 31.

23 Ibid., p. 33.

24 Ibid., p. 33.

25 See Sally Bloomfield, 'Spruiking Van Diemen's Land: The Long Reach of a Little Bushranger Book', *Script & Print*, 42:1 (2018), pp. 46–47.

26 Ibid., p. 83.

27 See Joseph Hall, *Virgidemiarum, Lib.I*, in Josiah Pratt, ed., *The Works of the Right Reverend Father in God, Joseph Hall*, Vol. 10 (C Whittingham: London: 1808), p. 283.

28 (Barron Field), 'Michael Howe, the last and worst of the Bush Rangers of Van Diemen's Land', *Quarterly Review*, Vol. 23, No. 45 (May 1820), p. 82.

29 *Michael Howe*, n.p.

30 Anon., 'Hobart Town', *Hobart Town Gazette and Van Diemen's Land Advertiser*, 18 August 1821, p. 2.

31 The playscript for this play no longer exists. The Allport Library and Museum of Fine Arts in Tasmania has a copy of the playbill for its October 1821 revival: see https://stors.tas.gov.au/144582715

32 David Burn, 'Van Diemen's Land', *Colonial Magazine*, 3 (September–December 1840), p. 364.

33 'Pindar Juvenal', *The Van Diemen's Land Warriors, or the Heroes of Cornwall; a Satire, in Three Cantos* (Launceston: Andrew Bent, 1827), p. 32.

34 Anon., 'Death of Donohoe', *Sydney Gazette and New South Wales Advertiser,* 4 September 1830, p. 2.

35 Anon., 'Australian Literature', *Sydney Monitor*, 10 May 1834, p. 2.

36 Charles Harpur, *The Bushrangers; a Play in Five Acts, and Other Poems* (Sydney: WR Piddington, 1853), p. 12.

37 Anon., 'Hobart Town', *Hobart Town Gazette*, 3 July 1819, p. 1.

38 Meg Foster, *Boundary Crossers: The Hidden History of Australia's Other Bushrangers* (Sydney: NewSouth Publishing, 2022), p. 94.

39 Ibid., p. 112.

40 Ibid., p. 109.

41 Ibid., p. 112.

42 Anon., 'Sydney', *Sydney Gazette and New South Wales Advertiser*, 19 May 1805, p. 2.

43 See Naomi Parry, '"Hanging No Good for Blackfellow": Looking into the Life of Musquito', in Ingereth Macfarlane and Mark Hannah, eds, *Transgressions: Critical Australian Indigenous Histories* (Canberra: ANU Press, 2007), p. 155.

44 Anon., 'Sydney', *Sydney Gazette and New South Wales Advertiser*, 11 August 1805, p. 2.
45 '"Hanging no good for blackfellow"', pp. 159–60.
46 Anon., 'Friday', *Hobart Town Gazette*, 20 August 1824, p. 2.
47 '"Hanging no good for blackfellow"', p. 161. A newspaper report in April 1825 noted that Tegg had not yet received a boat he was promised, although he was given some money. This may be why, for a short period, he 'absconded from the service of his employer' and joined a group of palawa people 'by whom many sanguinary acts of aggression have been subsequently perpetrated': Anon., 'Friday', *Hobart Town Gazette*, 15 April 1825, p. 2.
48 Ibid., p. 161. See also Kristyn Harman, *Aboriginal Convicts: Australian, Khoisan and Māori Exiles* (Sydney: UNSW Press, 2012), p. 35.
49 '"Hanging no good for blackfellow"', p. 160.
50 Charles Rowcroft, *Tales of the Colonies; or, The Adventures of an Emigrant* (London: Smith, Elder and Co., 1845), p. 100.
51 Ibid., p. 109.
52 Ibid., pp. 137–38.
53 Ibid., pp. 138–39.
54 Ibid., p. 206.
55 Ibid., p. 455.
56 Ibid., p. 447.
57 Ibid., p. 463.
58 Ibid., pp. 528–29.
59 Ibid., p. 523.
60 Martin Cash, *The Adventures of Martin Cash, comprising a faithful account of his exploits, while a bushranger under arms in Tasmania, in company with Kavanagh and Jones, in the year*

1843 (Hobart Town: Mercury Steam Press Office, 1870), p. 123. The ballad is sometimes attributed to the Irish convict poet (and bushranger) Frank McNamara, whom Cash had met at Port Arthur. But Philip Butterss suggests the author is actually James Lester Burke, who was also credited as the editor/compiler of Cash's autobiography: see Philip Butterss, 'James Lester Burke, Martin Cash and Frank the Poet', *Australian Literary Studies*, 15:3 (May 1992), pp. 220–26.

61 *The Adventures of Martin Cash*, p. 129.

62 'Peutetre', 'Colonial History: A Bushranger's Autobiography', *Australasian*, 1 February 1879, p. 8.

63 See 'Ned Kelly's Jerilderie Letter', National Museum of Australia.

64 See, for example, Michael Farrell, *Writing Unsettlement: Modes of Poetic Invention, 1796-1945* (New York: Palgrave Macmillan, 2015), pp. 13–38; and Ken Gelder and Rachael Weaver, *Colonial Australian Fiction: Character Types, Social Formations, and the Colonial Economy* (Sydney: Sydney University Press, 2017), pp. 56–58.

65 Ned Kelly, *The Jerilderie Letter* (Melbourne: Text Publishing, 2001), pp. 67–68.

66 Russel Ward, *The Australian Legend* (South Melbourne: Oxford University Press, 1958), p. 55.

67 Mark McKenna, *A History of Republicanism in Australia 1788-1996* (Cambridge: Cambridge University Press, 1996), p. 123.

68 Ned Kelly, *The Jerilderie Letter* (Melbourne: Text Publishing, 2001), p. 83.

69 George E Boxall, *History of the Australian Bushrangers* (London: T Fisher Unwin, 1908), p. 384.

70 Ibid., p. 385.

71 Ibid., p. 384.

72 David Carter and Roger Osborne, *Australian Books and Authors in the American Marketplace 1840s–1940s* (Sydney: Sydney University Press, 2018), pp. 41, 47.

73 Paul Eggert and Elizabeth Webby, eds, *Rolf Boldrewood, Robbery Under Arms* (St Lucia: University of Queensland Press, 2006), p. xxiv.

74 Peter Fritzsche, *Stranded in the Present: Modern Time and the Melancholy of History* (Cambridge, Mass.: Harvard University Press, 2004), pp. 211–12.

75 On Scott's 'neutral heroes', see, for example, Andrew Sanders, *The Victorian Historical Novel, 1840–1880* (Basingstoke: Macmillan, 1978), p. 9.

76 Rolf Boldrewood, *Robbery Under Arms*, Vol. 2 (Leipzig: Bernhard Tauchnitz, 1889), p. 347.

77 Rolf Boldrewood, *Robbery Under Arms* (London: Macmillan and Co., 1891), p. 394.

78 Robin Berwick Walker, 'The Historical Basis of *Robbery Under Arms*', *Australian Literary Studies*, 2:1 (1965), p. 5.

79 *Robbery Under Arms* (1891), p. 37.

80 Ibid., p. 301.

81 'Telemachus', 'A Good Australian Book', *Argus*, 18 January 1890, p. 4.

82 *Robbery Under Arms* (1891), p. 75.

83 Ibid., pp. 16, 134.

84 Ibid., p. 199.

85 Ibid., pp. 6, 65.

86 Ibid., pp. 38, 44.

87 Ibid., p. 171.

88 Ibid., p. 300.

89 'The Historical Basis of *Robbery Under Arms*', p. 4.

90 Rolf Boldrewood, *Old Melbourne Memories* (London: Macmillan and Co., Ltd., 1896), p. 41.

91 Ibid., p. 44.

92 Ibid., p. 66.

93 Jan Critchett, *Untold Stories: Memories and Lives of Victorian Kooris* (Melbourne: Melbourne University Press, 1998), p. 230.

94 *Old Melbourne Memories*, pp. 85–86.

95 Susan Margarey, *Passions of the First Wave Feminists* (Sydney: NewSouth Publishing, 2001), p. 44.

96 Mrs Campbell Praed, *Outlaw and Lawmaker,* Vol. 1 (London: Chatto & Windus, 1893), pp. 10, 19.

97 Ibid., p. 21.

98 See MJ Ryman, (1970) 'Genesis of a Colonial Secretary's Office: the Queensland Colonial Secretary's Office and its records, 1859-1898', *Archives & Manuscripts*, 4:2 (1970), p. 18.

99 Janette Gay Nolan, *Bundaberg History and People* (St Lucia: University of Queensland Press, 1978), p. 13.

100 *Outlaw and Lawmaker*, Vol. 1, p. 43.

101 Ibid., p. 43.

102 Ibid., p. 43.

103 Jonathan Richards, *The Secret War: A True History of Queensland's Native Police* (St Lucia: University of Queensland Press, 2008), p. 23.

104 Ibid., p. 63.

105 Legislative Assembly of NSW, *Report from the Select Committee on Murders by the Aborigines on the Dawson River* (Sydney: William Hanson, 1858), p. 113.

106 Rosa Praed, *Australian Life Black and White* (London: Chapman and Hall, 1885), p. 27.

107 Rosa Praed, *My Australian Girlhood: Sketches and Impressions of Bush Life* (London: T Fisher Unwin, 1902), pp. 91–92.

108 Ibid., pp. 91–92.

109 See Sigmund Freud, 'From the History of an Infantile Neurosis (1914, 1918), *Case Histories II: The Pelican Freud Library*, Vol. 9, trans. Angela Richards (Harmondsworth: Penguin, 1984), p. 294.

110 Patricia Clarke, 'Turning Fact into Fiction: The 1857 Hornet Bank Massacre', *Margin*, 65 (April 2005), p. 15.

111 Gordon Stephen Reid, *A Nest of Hornets: The Massacre of the Fraser Family at Hornet Bank Station, Central Queensland, 1857, and Related Events* (MA thesis, ANU, Feb 1981), p. 217.

112 *Outlaw and Lawmaker*, Vol. 3, p. 61.

113 Ibid., p. 56.

114 Ibid., pp. 61, 62.

115 Ibid., pp. 303–04.

Chapter 5

1 Gregory Blaxland, *Journal of a Tour of Discovery Across the Blue Mountains in New South Wales in 1823* (Sydney: Australian Historical Society, 1913), p. 39.

2 Ibid., p. 41.

3 For an excellent account of these events, see Stephen Gapps, *Gudyarra: The First Wiradyuri War of Resistance: the Bathurst War, 1822–1824* (Sydney: NewSouth Publishing, 2021).

4 John Oxley, *Journals of Two Expeditions into the Interior of New South Wales* (London: John Murray, 1820), p. 244.

5 Editorial, 'Sydney Gazette', *Sydney Gazette and New South Wales Advertiser,* 1 November 1831, p. 2.

6 Thomas Livingstone Mitchell, *Three Expeditions into the Interior of Eastern Australia*, Vol. 1 (London: T & W Boone, 1839), p. 2.

7 *Journals of Two Expeditions*, p. 284.

8 *Three Expeditions*, Vol. 1, p. 1.

9 Ibid., pp. 2, 34.
10 Ibid., p. 36.
11 Ibid., pp. 139–40.
12 Ibid., Vol. 2, p. 6.
13 Ibid., Vol. 1, p. 304.
14 Ibid., p. 274.
15 Ibid., Vol. 2, p. 101.
16 Ibid., pp. 102–03.
17 Editorial, 'Major Mitchell', *Sydney Gazette and New South Wales Advertiser*, 17 January 1837, p. 2.
18 Editorial, 'Expedition of Discovery', *Australian*, 8 November 1836, p. 2.
19 Editorial, 'Major Mitchell's Expedition', *Colonist*, 2 February 1837, p. 6.
20 Ibid., p. 8.
21 See *Supplement to the New South Wales Government Gazette*, No. 259, 21 January 1837, p. 62 , State Library Victoria.
22 *Three Expeditions*, Vol. 2, p. 94.
23 Ibid., p. 239.
24 Ibid., p. 76.
25 Ibid., p. 265.
26 Ibid., p. 266.
27 Ibid., p. 352.
28 Allison Cadzow, 'Ballandella (c. 1831–1863)', *Indigenous Australian Dictionary of Biography*, 2020.
29 Tiffany Shellam, *Meeting the Waylo: Aboriginal Encounters in the Archipelago* (Perth: UWA Publishing, 2019), p. 177.
30 For an account of Tupaia's role as an intermediary, see Anne Salmond, *The Trial of the Cannibal Dog*; and Kate Fullagar, *The Warrior, the Voyager, and the Artist: Three Lives in an Age of Empire* (New Haven: Yale University Press, 2020).

31 See Anon., 'The Western Australian Journal', *Perth Gazette and Western Australian Journal*, 12 July 1834, p. 318. Shellam mistakenly ascribes this passage to George Fletcher Moore, who contributed a diary entry on another topic in the next column of this newspaper. Moore did list the word Welo in his *Descriptive Vocabulary* (1842): see note 31, below. Moore had also heard about the shipwreck reported in the *Perth Gazette*, commenting in his *Diary of Ten Years of Eventful Life* (1884)—a chronicle of his life in Western Australia in the 1830s—about local rumours 'that "wayl-men" —men from a distance to the North' have spoken of it. He doesn't quite use the term Waylo here, although in a later entry he notes, interestingly, that 'the Perth natives' think 'that I speak like a Waylo man—that is, a man from the North'. See George Fletcher Moore, *Diary of Ten Years Eventful Life of an Early Settler in Western Australia* (London: M Walbrook, 1884), pp. 225, 262.

32 George Fletcher Moore, *A Descriptive Vocabulary of the Language in Common Use Amongst the Aborigines of Western Australia* (London: Wm S Orr & Co., 1842), p. 104.

33 John Lort Stokes, *Discoveries in Australia; with an Account of the Coasts and Rivers Explored and Surveyed During the Voyage of the H.M.S. Beagle, in the Years 1837-38-39-40-41-42-43*, Vol. 1 (London: T & W Boone, 1846), p. 75.

34 Ibid., pp. 91–92.

35 George Grey, *Journals of Two Expeditions of Discovery in North-West and Western Australia, During the Years 1837, 38, and 39*, Vol. 1 (London: T & W Boone, 1841), pp. 312–13.

36 Ibid., p. 2.

37 Ibid., p. 4.

38 Ibid., p. 67.

39 Ibid., p. 77.

40 Ibid., p. 80.
41 Ibid., p. 145.
42 Ibid., p. 147.
43 Ibid., p. 150.
44 Ibid., pp. 154–55.
45 Ibid., p. 155.
46 See, for example, Rachel Standfield, 'Introduction', in Rachel Standfield, ed., *Indigenous Mobilities: Across and Beyond the Antipodes* (Canberra: ANU Press, 2019), p. 9.
47 *Journals of Two Expeditions of Discovery*, p. 364.
48 Ibid., p. 365.
49 See George Grey, *A Vocabulary of the Dialects of South Western Australia* (London: T & W Boone, 1840), p. 126. It is worth adding that in 1845 Grey published an interesting map in the *Journal of the Royal Geographical Society of London* of what he thought at the time were the five primary Aboriginal dialects spoken in regions across the southern part of the continent, from Boorloo/Perth to Nerm/Port Phillip. His 'map of Aboriginal dialects' can be seen online at the State Library of South Australia.
50 *Journals of Two Expeditions*, Vol. 2, p. 365.
51 Ibid., p. 365.
52 Ibid., p. 75.
53 Ibid., p. 77.
54 Ibid., p. 25.
55 Ibid., p. 70.
56 Ibid., p. 70.
57 Ibid., p. 310.
58 Ibid., p. 310.
59 Clint Bracknell, 'The Emotional Business of Noongar Song', *Journal of Australian Studies*, 44:2 (2020), p. 144.

60 Anon., 'Ernest Favenc – Explorer. A Stirring Career', *Sydney Mail and New South Wales Advertiser*, 18 November 1908, p. 1310.

61 Ernest Favenc, *The History of Australian Exploration, from 1788 to 1888* (Sydney: Turner & Henderson, 1888), p. 121.

62 Ibid., p. v.

63 Robert Gouger, ed., *A Letter from Sydney, the Principal Town of Australasia* (London: Joseph Cross, 1829), p. 12.

64 Ibid., p. 12.

65 Jane Lydon, *Anti-Slavery and Australia*, p. 78.

66 Geoff Park, *Theatre Country: Essays on Landscape & Whenua* (Wellington: Victoria University Press, 2006), p. 37.

67 Thomas Walker, *A Month in the Bush of Australia. Journal of One of a Party of Gentlemen who Recently Travelled from Sydney to Port Philip* (London: J Cross, 1838), p. iv.

68 Ibid., p. v.

69 'Viator', 'Emigration', *Sydney Herald*, 19 September 1838, p. 4.

70 Thomas McCombie, *Arabin; or, the Adventures of a Colonist in New South Wales* (London: Simmonds & Ward, 1845), p. 6.

71 Ibid., p. 12.

72 Ibid., p. 74.

73 Ibid., p. 234.

74 Ibid., p. 68.

75 Ibid., p. 61.

76 Franco Moretti, *The Bourgeois*, p. 48.

77 *Arabin*, p. 112.

78 Ibid., p. 104.

79 John McLaren, *Dewigged, Bothered, and Bewildered: British Colonial Judges on Trial, 1800–1900* (Toronto: Osgoode Society for Canadian Legal History, 2011), p. 295.

80 *Arabin*, p. 225.

81 Ibid., p. 19.

82 Thomas McCombie, *Essays in Colonisation* (London: Smith, Elder, and Co., 1850), pp. 56, 83.

83 Ibid., p. 250.

84 Ibid., p. 76.

85 Ibid., p. 76.

86 Ibid., p. 76.

87 Ibid., p. 187.

88 In an otherwise interesting discussion of McCombie's novel, taking Arabin as an example of the 'settled subject' in colonial Australia, Philip Steer only fleetingly mentions this massacre: see Philip Steer, *Settler Colonialism in Victorian Literature: Economics and Political Identity in the Networks of Empire* (Cambridge: Cambridge University Press, 2020), pp. 51–57.

89 *Arabin*, p. 264.

90 Ibid., p. 269.

91 Ibid., pp. 270–71.

92 Michael F Christie, *Aborigines in Colonial Victoria, 1835–86*, (Sydney: Sydney University Press, 1979), p. 50.

93 Anon., 'Judicial Intelligence', *Port Phillip Gazette*, 2 August 1843, p. 3.

94 Ian D Clark, *Scars in the Landscape: A Register of Massacre Sites in Western Victoria* (Canberra: Aboriginal Studies Press, 1995), p. 41.

95 'Judicial Intelligence', p. 3.

96 *Scars in the Landscape*, p. 41.

97 *Essays in Colonisation*, p. 47.

98 Ibid., pp. 52, 55.

99 Anon., 'Review', *Eclectic Review*, 5 (February 1839), pp. 157, 183.

100 Ibid., p. 159.

101 Maria Weston Chapman, *Memorials of Harriet Martineau*, ed., Deborah A Logan (Lanham, Maryland: Lehigh University Press, 2015), p. 186.

102 See, for example, the 'Advertisement to the Third Edition' in 1860, which announced that the book 'was compiled by more than one person, all of whom are now not living': *The Southlanders: An Account of an Expedition to the Interior of New Holland* (London: John W Parker & Son, 1860), n.p. (Whately and Fox were both still alive in 1860, however.) A slightly different account is given in a letter written by a colleague of Whately's in June 1854, which notes that the book was 'written partly by the Archbishop of Dublin, and partly by some friends of his … [and] edited by Lady Mary Fox': see William John Fitzpatrick, *Memoirs of Richard Whately, Archbishop of Dublin*, Vol. 1 (London: Richard Bentley, 1864), p. 375.

103 Lady Mary Fox, ed., *Account of an Expedition to the Interior of New Holland* (London: Richard Bentley, 1837), p. 6.

104 Ibid., p. 12.

105 Ibid., p. 22.

106 Ibid., p. 134.

107 See Sumathi Ramaswamy, *The Lost Land of Lemuria: Fabulous Geographies, Catastrophic Histories* (Oakland, CA: University of California Press, 2004), p. 25. Philip Lutley Sclater's essay, 'The Mammals of Madagascar', was published in the *Quarterly Journal of Science* in 1864. Looking at the presence of lemurs in both Africa and India, it proposed a 'terrestrial connection' between the two, a 'faunal highway' across the Indian Ocean.

108 Ernest Haeckel, *The History of Creation, or The Development of the Earth and Its Inhabitants by the Action of Natural Causes*, Vol. 1, trans. E Ray Lankester (London: Henry S King, 1876), p. 361.

109 Andrew F Jones, *Developmental Fairy Tales: Evolutionary Thinking and Modern Chinese Culture* (Harvard, MA: Harvard University Press, 2011), p. 38.
110 See, for example, JJ Healy, 'The Lemurian Nineties', *Australian Literary Studies*, 8:3 (1978), pp. 307–16.
111 W Carlton Dawe, *The Golden Lake, or The Marvellous History of a Journey Through the Great Lone Land of Australia* (Melbourne, Sydney and Adelaide: EA Petherick & Co., 1891), p. 166.
112 Ibid., p. 272.
113 Ibid., p. 284.
114 Anon., 'Prospectus', *Sydney Morning Herald*, 17 July 1886, p. 5.
115 JD Hennessey, *An Australian Bush Track* (London: Sampson Low, Marston & Co., 1896), p. 4.
116 Ibid., pp. 12–13.
117 Ibid., p. 15.
118 John Hawkesworth, *An Account of the Voyages*, Vol. 3, p. 108.
119 Ibid., p. 108.
120 *An Australian Bush Track*, p. 110.
121 See John Bunyan, *The Pilgrim's Progress, from this World to that which is to Come* (London: Cassell, Petter, and Galpin, 1863), p. 390.
122 *An Australian Bush Track*, p. 210.
123 Ibid., p. 276.
124 Ibid., p. 253.
125 Ibid., p. 259.
126 Ibid., pp. 262, 311.
127 Ibid., p. 6.

Bibliography

Anderson, Stephanie, *Pelletier: The Forgotten Castaway of Cape York* (Melbourne: Melbourne Books, 2012).

Anon., 'A Magnificent Hoax', *Leader*, 29 October 1898, p. 21.

Anon., 'A Modern Munchausen', *Leader*, 8 October 1898, p. 21.

Anon., 'Australian Literature', *Sydney Monitor*, 10 May 1834, p. 2.

Anon., 'De Rougemont's "Wide World" Stories: The Two Tallest', *Brisbane Courier*, 12 November 1898, p. 2.

Anon., 'Death of Donohoe', *Sydney Gazette and New South Wales Advertiser*, 4 September 1830, p. 2.

Anon., 'Ernest Favenc – Explorer. A Stirring Career', *Sydney Mail and New South Wales Advertiser*, 18 November 1908, p. 1310.

Anon., 'Fatal Excursion', *Sydney Gazette and New South Wales Advertiser*, 26 June 1803, p. 4.

Anon., 'Friday', *Hobart Town Gazette*, 15 April 1825, p. 2.

Anon., 'Friday', *Hobart Town Gazette*, 20 August 1824, p. 2.

Anon., 'Fugitives', *Sydney Gazette and New South Wales Advertiser*, 5 March 1803, p. 3.

Anon., 'Hobart Town', *Hobart Town Gazette and Van Diemen's Land Advertiser*, 18 August 1821, p. 2.

Anon., 'Hobart Town', *Hobart Town Gazette*, 12 April 1817, p. 2.

Anon., 'Hobart Town', *Hobart Town Gazette*, 3 July 1819, p. 1.

Anon., 'Judicial Intelligence', *Port Phillip Gazette*, 2 August 1843, p. 3.

Anon., 'Parramatta', *Sydney Gazette and New South Wales Advertiser*, 17 February 1805, p. 2.

Anon., 'Prospectus', *Sydney Morning Herald*, 17 July 1886, p. 5.

Anon., 'Review', *Eclectic Review*, 5 February 1839, pp. 157–85.

Anon., *Supplement to the New South Wales Government Gazette*, No. 259, 21 January 1837, State Library Victoria.

Anon., 'Sydney', *Sydney Gazette and New South Wales Advertiser*, 19 June 1806, p. 1.

Anon., 'Sydney Gazette', *Sydney Gazette and New South Wales Advertiser*, 2 March 1806, p. 2.

Anon., 'Sydney', *Sydney Gazette and New South Wales Advertiser*, 11 August 1805, p. 2.

Anon., 'Sydney', *Sydney Gazette and New South Wales Advertiser*, 19 May 1805, p. 2.

Anon., 'The Daphne Case', *Queenslander*, 9 October 1869, p. 9.

Anon., *The Life and Surprising Adventures of Blue-Eyed Patty, The Valiant Female Soldier* (c.1790), State Library of New South Wales collection.

Anon., 'The Rougemont Romance', *Daily Telegraph*, 27 October 1898, p. 3.

Anon., *The Travels of Hildebrand Bowman* (London: W Strahan and T Cadell, 1778).

Anon., 'The Western Australian Journal', *Perth Gazette and Western Australian Journal*, 12 July 1834, p. 318.

Anon., 'William Buckley', *Age*, 29 July 1911, p. 4.

Banivanua-Mar, Tracey, *Violence and Colonial Dialogue: The Australian-Pacific Indentured Labour Trade* (Honolulu: University of Hawai'i Press, 2007).

Barnes, Geraldine, 'Curiosity, Wonder, and William Dampier's Painted Prince', *Journal for Early Modern Cultural Studies*, 6:1 (Spring–Summer 2006), pp. 31–50.

Beck, Ulrich, 'The Cosmopolitan Perspective: Sociology in the Second Age of Modernity', in Steven Vertovec and Robin Cohen, eds, *Conceiving Cosmopolitanism: Theory, Context, and Practice* (Oxford: Oxford University Press, 2002).

Becke, Louis, 'Collier: The "Blackbirder"', *Pacific Tales* (Philadelphia: JB Lippincott Company, 1896).

Becke, Louis, 'The Wreck of the Leonora: A Memory of "Bully" Hayes', *Ridan the Devil and Other Stories* (Philadelphia: JB Lippincott Company, 1899).

Behrendt, Larissa, *Finding Eliza: Power and Colonial Storytelling* (St Lucia: University of Queensland Press, 2016).

Bertelsen, Lance, 'Introduction', *The Travels of Hildebrand Bowman* (Peterborough, Ontario: Broadview Press, 2017).

Bladen, FM, ed., *Historical Records of New South Wales – Phillip, 1783-1792*, Vol. 1, Part 2 (Sydney: Charles Potter, Government Printer, 1892).

Bladen, FM, ed., *Historical Records of New South Wales – Hunter, 1796-1799*, Vol. 3 (Sydney: Charles Potter, Government Printer, 1895).

Blaxland, Gregory, *Journal of a Tour of Discovery Across the Blue Mountains in New South Wales in 1823* (Sydney: Australian Historical Society, 1913).

Bloomfield, Sally, 'Spruiking Van Diemen's Land: The Long Reach of a Little Bushranger Book', *Script & Print,* 42:1 (2018), pp. 26–47.

Bodek, Richard and Kelly, Joseph, eds, *Maroons and the Marooned: Runaways and Castaways in the Americas* (Jackson, US: University Press of Mississippi, 2020).

Boldrewood, Rolf, *Old Melbourne Memories* (London: Macmillan and Co., Ltd., 1896).

Boldrewood, Rolf, *Robbery Under Arms* (Leipzig: Bernhard Tauchnitz, 1889).

Boldrewood, Rolf, *Robbery Under Arms* (London: Macmillan and Co., 1891).

Boxall, George E, *History of the Australian Bushrangers* (London: T Fisher Unwin, 1908).

Boyce, James, *Van Diemen's Land* (Melbourne: Black Inc., 2018).

Bracknell, Clint, 'The Emotional Business of Noongar Song', *Journal of Australian Studies*, 44:2 (2020), pp. 140–53.

Brierly, OW, 'Journals of H.M.S. Rattlesnake', in David R Moore, *Islanders and Aborigines at Cape York: An Ethnographic Reconstruction Based on the 1848-1850* Rattlesnake *Journals of O.W. Brierly and Information He Obtained from Barbara Thompson* (Canberra; Australian Institute of Aboriginal Studies, 1979).

Brook, Jack, 'The Widow and the Child', *Aboriginal History*, 12:1–2 (1988), pp. 63–78.

Buckley, William, *Reminiscences of James* [sic] *Buckley Who Lived for Thirty Years Among the Wallawarro or Watourong Tribes at Geelong Port Phillip, communicated by him to George Langhorne, 1837*, State Library of Victoria's Manuscripts Collection.

Bunyan, John, *The Pilgrim's Progress, from this World to that which is to Come* (London: Cassell, Petter, and Galpin, 1863).

Burn, David, 'Van Diemen's Land', *Colonial Magazine*, 3 (September–December 1840), pp. 353–64.

Burnard, Trevor and Garrigus, John, *The Plantation Machine: Atlantic Capitalism in French Saint-Domingue and British Jamaica* (Philadelphia: University of Pennsylvania Press, 2016).

Butterss, Philip, 'James Lester Burke, Martin Cash and Frank the Poet', *Australian Literary Studies*, 15: 3 (May 1992), pp. 220–26.

Byron, John, *The Narrative of the Honourable John Byron* (London: S Baker and G Leigh, 1768).

Byron, John, *A Voyage Round the World, in His Majesty's Ship The* Dolphin (London: J Newberry and F Newberry, 1868).

Cadzow, Allison, 'Ballandella (c. 1831–1863)', *Indigenous Australian Dictionary of Biography*, 2020: https://adb.anu.edu.au/biography/ballandella-30144/text37019

Carey, Daniel, 'Reading Contrapuntally: *Robinson Crusoe*, Slavery, and Postcolonial Theory', in Daniel Carey and Lynn Festa, eds, *The Postcolonial Enlightenment: Eighteenth-Century Colonialism and Postcolonial Theory* (Oxford: Oxford University Press, 2009).

Carnegie DW, *Grien on Rougemont; or the Story of a Modern Robinson Crusoe* (London: Edward Lloyd, Ltd. [*Daily Chronicle*], 1898).

Carter, David and Osborne, Roger, *Australian Books and Authors in the American Marketplace 1840s–1940s* (Sydney: Sydney University Press, 2018).

Carter, Paul, *The Road to Botany Bay: An Exploration of Landscape and History* (Minneapolis: University of Minnesota Press, 2010).

Cash, Martin, *The Adventures of Martin Cash, comprising a faithful account of his exploits, while a bushranger under arms in Tasmania, in company with Kavanagh and Jones, in the year 1843* (Hobart Town: Mercury Steam Press Office, 1870).

Castiglia, Christopher, *Bound and Determined: Captivity, Culture-Crossing, and White Womanhood from Mary Rowlandson to Patty Hearst* (Chicago: University of Chicago Press, 1996).

Causer, Tim, 'Introduction', in Tim Causer, Margot Finn and Philip Schofield, eds, *Jeremy Bentham and Australia: Convicts, Utility and Empire* (London: UCL Press, 2022).

Causer, Tim, ed., *Memorandoms by James Martin: An Astonishing Escape from Early New South Wales* (London: UCL Press, 2017).

Chapman, Maria Weston, *Memorials of Harriet Martineau*, ed., Deborah A Logan (Lanham, Maryland: Lehigh University Press, 2015).

Christie, Michael F, *Aborigines in Colonial Victoria, 1835–86*, (Sydney: Sydney University Press, 1979).

Christopher, Emma, 'From the Caribbean to Queensland: Re-examining Australia's "Blackbirding" Past and its Roots in the Global Slave Trade', *Conversation*, 4 June 2021.

Christopher, Emma, '"The Slave Trade is Merciful Compared to [This]": Slave Traders, Convict Transportation, and the Abolitionists', in Emma Christopher, Cassandra Pybus and Marcus Rediker, eds, *Many Middle Passages: Forced Migration and the Making of the Modern World* (Berkeley: University of California Press, 2007).

Clark, Ian D, *Scars in the Landscape: A Register of Massacre Sites in Western Victoria* (Canberra: Aboriginal Studies Press, 1995).

Clarke, Marcus, *For the Term of His Natural Life* (London: Richard Bentley, 1886).

Clarke, Patricia, 'Turning Fact into Fiction: The 1857 Hornet Bank Massacre', *Margin*, 65 (April 2005), pp. 8–17.

Cobbold, Richard, *The History and Extraordinary Adventures of Margaret Catchpole, A Suffolk Girl* (New York: D Appleton & Co., 1846).

Collins, David, *An Account of the English Colony in New South Wales* (London: T Cadell and W Davies, 1798).

Critchett, Jan, *Untold Stories: Memories and Lives of Victorian Kooris* (Melbourne: Melbourne University Press, 1998).

Curthoys, Ann and Mitchell, Jessie, *Taking Liberty: Indigenous Rights and Settler Self-Government in Colonial Australia, 1830-1890* (Cambridge: Cambridge University Press, 2018).

Curtis, John, *Shipwreck of the Stirling Castle* (London: George Virtue, 1838).

Dampier, William, *A New Voyage Round the World* (London: James Knapton, 1699).

Dampier, William, *A Voyage to New Holland* (London: James Knapton, 1703).

Darian-Smith, Kate, et al., *Captured Lives: Australian Captivity Narratives* (London: Sir Robert Menzies Centre for Australian Studies, 1992).

Darian-Smith, Kate, '"Rescuing" Barbara Thompson and other white women: captivity narratives on Australian frontiers', in Kate Darian-Smith, Liz Gunner and Sarah Nuttall, eds, *Text, Theory, Space : Land, Literature, and History in South Africa and Australia* (London: Routledge, 1996).

Davies, John, trans., *The History of the Caribby-Islands* (London: Thomas Dring and John Starkey, 1666).

Dawe, W Carlton, *The Golden Lake, or The Marvellous History of a Journey Through the Great Lone Land of Australia* (Melbourne, Sydney and Adelaide: EA Petherick & Co., 1891).

Dawson, James, *Australian Aborigines: The Languages and Customs of Several Tribes of Aborigines in the Western District of Victoria, Australia* (Melbourne: George Robertson, 1881).

de Foigny, Gabriel, *A New Discovery of Terra Incognita Australia, or the Southern World, by James Sadeur, a French-man* (London: John Dunton, 1693).

de Patot, Simon Tyssot, *The Travels and Adventures of James Massey* (London: John Watts, 1733).

de Rougemont, Louis, *The Adventures of Louis de Rougemont, As Told by Himself* (London: George Newnes, Ltd., 1899).

Defoe, Daniel, *The Life and Strange Surprizing Adventures of Robinson Crusoe* (London: W Taylor, 1719).

Dickens, Charles, *Great Expectations* (London: Chapman and Hall, 1862).

Dortins, Emma, *The Lives of Stories: Three Aboriginal settler Friendships* (ANU Press 2018).

Duffield, Ian, 'Martin Beck and Afro-Blacks in Colonial Australia', *Journal of Australian Studies*, 9:16 (1985), pp. 3–20.

Duffield, Ian, 'Cutting Out and Taking Liberties: Australia's Convict Pirates, 1790–1829', *International Review of Social History*, 58 (December 2013), pp. 197–227.

Editorial, 'Expedition of Discovery', *Australian*, 8 November 1836, p. 2.

Editorial, 'Major Mitchell', *Sydney Gazette and New South Wales Advertiser*, 17 January 1837, p. 2.

Editorial, 'Major Mitchell's Expedition', *Colonist*, 2 February 1837, p. 6.

Editorial, 'Sydney Gazette', *Sydney Gazette and New South Wales Advertiser*, 1 November 1831, p. 2.

Edminson, Mary, 'The Date of the Action in *Great Expectations*', *Nineteenth-Century Fiction*, 13 (June 1958), pp. 22–35.

Edmonds, Penelope and Nettelbeck, Amanda, eds, *Intimacies of Violence in the Settler Colony* (Basingstoke: Palgrave, 2018).

Edwards, Philip, *The Story of the Voyage: Sea-Narratives in Eighteenth-Century England* (Cambridge: Cambridge University Press, 1994).

Edwards, Sophia, *Surprising Misfortunes of Sophia Johnson. Written by Herself* (Chester: J Williams, 1838), National Library of Australia.

Eggert, Paul and Webby, Elizabeth, eds, *Rolf Boldrewood, Robbery Under Arms* (St Lucia: University of Queensland Press, 2006).

Farrell, Michael, *Writing Unsettlement: Modes of Poetic Invention, 1796-1945* (New York: Palgrave Macmillan, 2015).

Favenc, Ernest, *The History of Australian Exploration, from 1788 to 1888* (Sydney: Turner & Henderson, 1888).

Ferguson, Frances, *Pornography, the Theory* (Chicago: University of Chicago Press, 2004).

Field, Barron (?), 'Michael Howe, the Last and Worst of the Bush Rangers of Van Diemen's Land', *Quarterly Review*, Vol. 23, No. 45 (May 1820), pp. 73–83.

Fitzgerald, William G, 'Introduction', *Wide World Magazine*, Vol. 1, No. 1 (May 1898), p. 3.

Fitzgerald, William G, 'The Adventures of Louis de Rougemont', *Wide World Magazine*, Vol. 1, No. 5 (September 1898).

Fitzpatrick, William John, *Memoirs of Richard Whately, Archbishop of Dublin* (London: Richard Bentley, 1864).

Flynn, Michael, 'Second Fleet', *The Dictionary of Sydney*, 2016.

Forster, George, *A Voyage Round the World*, Vol. II (London: B White, J Robson, P Elmsly and G Robinson, 1777).

Foster, Meg, *Boundary Crossers: The Hidden History of Australia's Other Bushrangers* (Sydney: NewSouth Publishing, 2022).

Fox, Lady Mary, ed. (?), *Account of an Expedition to the Interior of New Holland* (London: Richard Bentley, 1837).

Fox, Lady Mary, ed. (?), *The Southlanders: An Account of an Expedition to the Interior of New Holland* (London: John W Parker & Son, 1860).

Fraser, Eliza, *Narrative of the Capture, Sufferings, and Miraculous Escape of Mrs Eliza Fraser* (New York: Charles S Webb, 1837).

Freud, Sigmund, 'From the History of an Infantile Neurosis (1914, 1918)', *Case Histories II: The Pelican Freud Library*, Vol. 9, trans. Angela Richards (Harmondsworth: Penguin, 1984).

Fritzsche, Peter, *Stranded in the Present: Modern Time and the Melancholy of History* (Cambridge, Mass.: Harvard University Press, 2004).

Fuchs, Barbara, *Knowing Fictions: Picaresque Reading in the Early Modern Hispanic World* (Philadelphia: University of Pennsylvania Press, 2021).

Fullagar, Kate, *The Savage Visit: New World People and Popular Imperial Culture in Britain, 1710–1795* (Berkeley, CA: University of California Press, 2012).

Gapps, Stephen, *Gudyarra: The First Wiradyuri War of Resistance: the Bathurst War, 1822–1824* (Sydney: NewSouth Publishing, 2021).

Gapps, Stephen, *The Sydney Wars* (Sydney: NewSouth Publishing, 2018).

Gelder, Ken and Weaver, Rachael, *Colonial Australian Fiction: Character Types, Social Formations, and the Colonial Economy* (Sydney: Sydney University Press, 2017).

George Barrington (?), *History of New South Wales, including Botany Bay, Port Jackson, Parramatta, Sydney, and All its Dependencies* (London: M Jones, 1802).

Gibbings, Robert, *John Graham, Convict, 1824* (1937; London: John Dent, 1956).

Gibson, Ross, *Seven Versions of an Australian Badland* (St Lucia: University of Queensland Press, 2002).

Gibson, Ross, *The Diminishing Paradise: Changing Literary Perceptions of Australia* (Sydney: Angus & Robertson, 1984).

Giles, Paul, 'The Global Invention of the Australian Novel', in David Carter, ed., *The Cambridge History of the Australian Novel* (Cambridge: Cambridge University Press, 2023).

Gill, Sam D, *Storytracking: Texts, Stories & Histories in Central Australia* (Oxford: Oxford University Press, 1998).

Gillen, Mollie, Browning, Yvonne and Flynn, Michael *The Founders of Australia: A Biographical Dictionary of the First Fleet* (Australia: Library of Australian History, 1989).

Gouger, Robert, ed., *A Letter from Sydney, the Principal Town of Australasia* (London: Joseph Cross, 1829).

Grey, George, *A Vocabulary of the Dialects of South Western Australia* (London: T & W Boone, 1840).

Grey, George, *Journals of Two Expeditions of Discovery in North-West and Western Australia, During the Years 1837, 38, and 39* (London: T & W Boone, 1841).

Grove Day, A., *Louis Becke* (Melbourne: Hill of Content, 1967), p. 148.

Haeckel, Ernest, *The History of Creation, or The Development of the Earth and Its Inhabitants by the Action of Natural Causes*, Vol. 1, trans. E Ray Lankester (London: Henry S King, 1876).

Hall, Joseph, *Virgidemiarum, Lib.I*, in Josiah Pratt, ed., *The Works of the Right Reverend Father in God, Joseph Hall*, Vol. 10 (C Whittingham: London: 1808).

Harman, Kristyn, *Aboriginal Convicts: Australian, Khoisan and Māori Exiles* (Sydney: UNSW Press, 2012).

Harpur, Charles, *The Bushrangers; a Play in Five Acts, and Other Poems* (Sydney: WR Piddington, 1853).

Harris, Alexander, *Martin Beck; or, The Story of an Australian Settler* (London: G Routledge and Co., 1852).

Haskins, Victoria K, 'Women's Work and Cross-Cultural Relationships on Two Female Frontiers: Eliza Fraser and Barbara Thompson in Colonial Queensland, 1836-1849', in Penelope Edmonds and Amanda Nettelbeck, eds, *Intimacies of Violence in the Settler Colony* (Basingstoke: Palgrave, 2018).

Hawkesworth, John, *An Account of the Voyages Undertaken by the Order of His Present Majesty for Making Discoveries in the Southern Hemisphere* (London: W Strahan and T Cadell, 1773).

Healy, JJ, 'The Lemurian Nineties', *Australian Literary Studies*, 8:3 (1978), pp. 307–16.

Hennessey, JD, *An Australian Bush Track* (London: Sampson Low, Marston & Co., 1896).

Hergenhan, Laurie, *Unnatural Lives: Studies in Australian Fiction about the Convicts, from James Tucker to Patrick White* (St Lucia: University of Queensland Press, 1983).

Hobbes, Thomas, *Leviathan* (Oxford: Oxford University Press, 1901).

Hogan, James Francis, ed., *The Convict King, Being the Life and Adventures of Jorgen Jorgenson* (London: Ward & Downey, 1891).

Howell, John, *The Life and Adventures of Alexander Selkirk* (Edinburgh: Oliver & Boyd, 1829).

Howitt, William, *The History of Discovery in Australia, Tasmania, and New Zealand*, Vol. 1 (London: Longman, Green, Longman, Roberts, and Green, 1865).

Huber, Therese, *Adventures on a Journey to New Holland*, trans. Rodney Livingstone (Melbourne: Lansdowne Press, 1966).

Jackman, William, *The Australian Captive; or, An Authentic Narrative of Fifteen Years in the Life of William Jackman* (Auburn, USA: Derby and Miller, 1853).

Jones, Andrew F, *Developmental Fairy Tales: Evolutionary Thinking and Modern Chinese Culture* (Harvard, MA: Harvard University Press, 2011).

Jorgenson, Jorgen, 'A Shred of Autobiography', *Hobart Town Almanack and Van Diemen's Annual* (Hobart Town: James Ross, 1835).

Jorgenson, Jorgen, 'Original Correspondence', *Hobart Town Advertiser*, 31 June 1840, p. 2.

Joyce, James, 'Daniel Defoe', trans. Joseph Prescott, *Buffalo Studies*, 1 (1964), pp. 12–24.

Juvenal, Pindar, *The Van Diemen's Land Warriors, or the Heroes of Cornwall; a Satire, in Three Cantos* (Launceston: Andrew Bent, 1827).

Karskens, Grace, *People of the River: Lost Worlds of Early Australia* (Sydney: Allen & Unwin, 2020).

Karskens, Grace, '"This Spirit of Emigration": The Nature and Meanings of Escape in Early New South Wales', *Journal of Australian Colonial History*, 7 (2005), pp. 19–22.

Kelly, Ned, *The Jerilderie Letter* (Melbourne: Text Publishing, 2001).

Keynes, RD, *Charles Darwin's Beagle Diary* (Cambridge: Cambridge University Press, 1988).

Kibberd, Declan, *Irish Classics* (Cambridge, MA: Harvard University Press, 2001).

Konishi, Shino, *The Aboriginal Male in the Enlightenment World* (London: Taylor & Francis, 2015).

Lang, John Dunmore, *Transportation and Colonisation* (London: AJ Valpy, 1837).

Legislative Assembly of NSW, *Report from the Select Committee on Murders by the Aborigines on the Dawson River* (Sydney: William Hanson, 1858).

Levine, Donald N., ed., *Georg Simmel: On Individuality and Social Forms* (Chicago: University of Chicago Press, 1971).

Lydon, Jane, *Anti-Slavery and Australia: No Slavery in a Free Land?* (London and New York: Routledge, 2021).

MacGillivray, John, *Narrative of the Voyage of H.M.S. Rattlesnake*, Vol. 1 (London: T & W Boone, 1852).

Macintyre, Stuart, *A Concise History of Australia* (Cambridge: Cambridge University Press, 2004).

Mackaness, George, ed., *Michael Howe: The Last & Worst of the Bush-rangers of Van Diemen's Land* (Exile Bay: ETT Imprint, 2021).

Maconochie, Alexander, *Australiana: Thoughts on Convict Management and Other Subjects Connected with the Australian Penal Colonies* (London: John W Parker, 1839).

Malouf, David, *Remembering Babylon* (London: Vintage, 1993).

Manjapra, Kris, *Colonialism in Global Perspective* (Cambridge: Cambridge University Press, 2020).

Margarey, Susan, *Passions of the First Wave Feminists* (Sydney: NewSouth Publishing, 2001).

Maynard, John and Haskins, Victoria K, *Living with the Locals: Early Europeans' Experience of Indigenous Life* (Canberra: National Library of Australia, 2016).

McCombie, Thomas, *Arabin; or, the Adventures of a Colonist in New South Wales* (London: Simmonds & Ward, 1845).

McCombie, Thomas, *Essays in Colonisation* (London: Smith, Elder, and Co., 1850).

McKenna, Mark, *A History of Republicanism in Australia 1788-1996* (Cambridge: Cambridge University Press, 1996).

McLaren, John, *Dewigged, Bothered, and Bewildered: British Colonial Judges on Trial, 1800–1900* (Toronto: Osgoode Society for Canadian Legal History, 2011).

McMorran, Will, 'The Marquis de Sade in English, 1800–1850', *Modern Language Review*, 112:3 (July 2017), pp. 549–66.

Meredith, David and Oxley, Deborah, 'The Convict Economy', in Simon Ville and Glenn Withers, eds, *The Cambridge Economic History of Australia* (Cambridge: Cambridge University Press, 2014).

Miller, E Morris, *Australia's First Two Novels: Origins and Backgrounds* (Hobart: Tasmanian Historical Research Association, 1958).

Miller, Olga, 'K-gari, Mrs Fraser and Butchulla Oral Tradition', in Ian J McNiven, Lynette Russell and Kay Schaffer, eds, *Constructions of Colonialism: Perspectives on Eliza Fraser's Shipwreck* (London and New York: Leicester University Press, 1998).

Mitchell, Adrian, *Dampier's Monkey* (Adelaide: Wakefield Press, 2010).

Mitchell, Thomas Livingstone, *Three Expeditions into the Interior of Eastern Australia*, Vol. 1 (London: T & W Boone, 1839).

Moore, George Fletcher, *A Descriptive Vocabulary of the Language in Common Use Amongst the Aborigines of Western Australia* (London: Wm S Orr & Co., 1842).

Moore, George Fletcher, *Diary of Ten Years Eventful Life of an Early Settler in Western Australia* (London: M Walbrook, 1884).

Moretti, Franco, *The Bourgeois: Between History and Literature* (London and New York: Verso, 2013).

Morgan, John, *The Life and Adventures of William Buckley* (Hobart: Archibald MacDougall, 1852).

Mountford, Benjamin, *Britain, China, and Colonial Australia* (Oxford: Oxford University Press, 2016).

Nettelbeck, Amanda, 'From Humanitarianism to Humane Governance: Aboriginal Slavery and White Australia', in Joy Damousi, Trevor Burnard and Alan Lester, eds, *Humanitarianism, Empire and Transnationalism, 1760-1995: Selective Humanity in the Anglophone World* (Manchester: Manchester University Press, 2022).

Nettelbeck, Amanda and Foster, Robert, *In the Name of the Law: William Willshire and the Policing of the Australian Frontier* (Adelaide: Wakefield Press, 2007).

Neville, Henry, *The Isle of Pines; or a Late Discovery of a Fourth Island, in Terra Australia Incognita* (London: T Cadell, 1668).

Nicol, John, *The Life and Adventures of John Nicol, Mariner* (Edinburgh: Blackwood, 1822).

Nolan, Janette Gay, *Bundaberg History and People* (St Lucia: University of Queensland Press, 1978).

O'Connell, Lisa, 'Before *Frankenstein*: Therese Huber and the Antipodean Emergence of Political Fiction', *Postcolonial Studies*, 23:3 (2020), pp. 348–59.

Oxley, John, *Journals of Two Expeditions into the Interior of New South Wales* (London: John Murray, 1820).

Palmer, George, *Kidnapping in the South Seas; Being a Narrative of a Three Months' Cruise of H.M. Ship Rosario* (Edinburgh: Edmonston and Douglas, 1871).

Palmer, George, letter to the Crown Solicitor, 16 August 1869, *New South Wales. Notes and Proceedings of the Legislative Assembly During the Session of 1871-2*, Vol. 1 (Sydney: Thomas Richards, Government Printer, 1872).

Park, Geoff, *Theatre Country: Essays on Landscape & Whenua* (Wellington: Victoria University Press, 2006).

Parry, Naomi, '"Hanging No Good for Blackfellow": Looking into the Life of Musquito', in Ingereth Macfarlane and Mark Hannah, eds, *Transgressions: Critical Australian Indigenous Histories* (Canberra: ANU Press, 2007).

Petram, Lodewijk, *The World's First Stock Exchange*, trans. Lynne Richards (New York: Columbia University Press, 2014).

Petrie, Constance Campbell, *Tom Petrie's Reminiscences of Early Queensland* (Brisbane: Watson, Ferguson & Co., 1904).

'Peutetre', 'Colonial History: A Bushranger's Autobiography', *Australasian*, 1 February 1879, p. 8.

Porter, James, 'A Narrative of the Sufferings and Adventures of Certain of the Ten Convicts, Who Piratically Seized the Brig "Frederick" at Macquarie Harbour, in Van Diemen's Land ...', *The Hobart Town Almanack and Van Diemen's Land Annual* (Hobart Town: William Gore Elliston, 1838).

Porter, James, *Autobiography of convict James Porter, written on Norfolk Island 1840-1844*, State Library of New South Wales.

Praed, Rosa, *Australian Life Black and White* (London: Chapman and Hall, 1885).

Praed, Rosa, *Outlaw and Lawmaker* (London: Chatto & Windus, 1893).

Praed, Rosa, *My Australian Girlhood: Sketches and Impressions of Bush Life* (London: T Fisher Unwin, 1902).

Pybus, Cassandra, *Black Founders: The Unknown Story of Australia's First Black Settlers* (Sydney: UNSW Press, 2006).

Ramaswamy, Sumathi, *The Lost Land of Lemuria: Fabulous Geographies, Catastrophic Histories* (Oakland, CA: University of California Press, 2004).

Reid, Gordon Stephen, *A Nest of Hornets: The Massacre of the Fraser Family at Hornet Bank Station, Central Queensland, 1857, and Related Events* (MA thesis, ANU, Feb 1981).

Richards, Jonathan, *The Secret War: A True History of Queensland's Native Police* (St Lucia: University of Queensland Press, 2008).

Robinson, Cedric J, *Black Marxism* (Chapel Hill: University of North Carolina Press, 2000).

Rowcroft, Charles, *Tales of the Colonies; or, The Adventures of an Emigrant* (London: Smith, Elder and Co., 1845).

Ryan, JS, 'The Several Fates of Eliza Fraser', *Journal of the Royal Historical Society of Queensland*, 11: 4 (1981), pp. 88–112.

Ryman, MJ, 'Genesis of a Colonial Secretary's Office: the Queensland Colonial Secretary's Office and its records, 1859-1898', *Archives & Manuscripts*, 4:2 (1970), pp. 17–30.

Salmond, Anne, *The Trial of the Cannibal Dog* (New Haven: Yale University Press, 2003).

Sanders, Andrew, *The Victorian Historical Novel, 1840–1880* (Basingstoke: Macmillan, 1978).

Savery, Henry, *Quintus Servinton. A Tale Founded Upon Incidents of Real Occurrence* (Hobart Town: Henry Melville, 1830).

Schaffer, Kay, *In the Wake of First Contact: The Eliza Fraser Stories* (Cambridge: Cambridge University Press, 1995).

Shellam, Tiffany, *Meeting the Waylo: Aboriginal Encounters in the Archipelago* (Perth: UWA Publishing, 2019).

Shillinglaw, John, 'Review', *Herald*, 9 May 1874, p. 3.

Smith, Bernard, *European Vision and the South Pacific* (1959; Melbourne: The Miegunyah Press, 2022).

Spicer, Chrystopher John, 'The Granite and the Rainbow: Towards a New Biography of Louis Becke', *Journal of the Association for the Study of Australian Literature,* 21:2 (2021).

Standfield, Rachel, 'Introduction', in Rachel Standfield, ed., *Indigenous Mobilities: Across and Beyond the Antipodes* (Canberra: ANU Press, 2019).

Steer, Philip, *Settler Colonialism in Victorian Literature: Economics and Political Identity in the Networks of Empire* (Cambridge: Cambridge University Press, 2020).

Stokes, John Lort, *Discoveries in Australia; with an Account of the Coasts and Rivers Explored and Surveyed During the Voyage of the H.M.S. Beagle, in the Years 1837-38-39-40-41-42-43,* Vol. 1 (London: T & W Boone, 1846).

Stuart, Lurline, ed., *Marcus Clarke, His Natural Life* (St Lucia: University of Queensland Press, 2001).

Swift, Jonathan, *Travels into Several Remote Nations of the World, By Captain Lemuel Gulliver*, Vol. 2 (London: Benjamin Motte, 1726).

Taylor, Rebe, *Unearthed: The Aboriginal Tasmanians of Kangaroo Island* (Adelaide: Wakefield Press, 2008).

'Telemachus', 'A Good Australian Book', *Argus*, 18 January 1890, p. 4.

Tench, Watkin, *A Complete Account of the Settlement at Port Jackson, in New South Wales* (London: G Nicol and J Sewell, 1793).

Thomas, Nicholas and Berghof, Oliver, eds, *A Voyage Round the World: George Forster*, Vol. 1 (Honolulu: University of Hawai'I Press, 2000).

Thomas, Nicholas, *Cook: The Extraordinary Voyages of Captain James Cook* (New York: Walker & Company, 2003).

Tucker, James (?), *The Adventures of Ralph Rashleigh: A Penal Exile in Australia, 1825-1844* (Hawthorn, Victoria: Lloyd O'Neill, 1970).

'Viator', 'Emigration', *Sydney Herald*, 19 September 1838, p. 4.

Walker, James Backhouse, ed., *Abel Janszoon Tasman: His Life and Voyages* (Hobart: William Grahame Jr., 1896).

Walker, Robin Berwick, 'The Historical Basis of *Robbery Under Arms*', *Australian Literary Studies*, 2:1 (1965), pp. 3–14.

Walker, Thomas, *A Month in the Bush of Australia. Journal of One of a Party of Gentlemen who Recently Travelled from Sydney to Port Philip* (London: J Cross, 1838).

Ward, Russel, *The Australian Legend* (South Melbourne: Oxford University Press, 1958).

Whately, Richard, *Remarks on Transportation, and on a Recent Defence of the System* (London: B Fellowes, 1834).

Williams, Glyndwr, *The Great South Sea: English Voyages and Encounters, 1570–1750* (New Haven: Yale University Press, 1997).

Willshire, WH, *A Thrilling Tale of Real Life in the Wilds of Australia* (Adelaide: Frearson and Brother, 1895).

Woollacott, Angela, *Gender and Empire* (Basingstoke: Palgrave, 2006).

Wright, Christine, *Wellington's Men in Australia: Peninsular War Veterans and the Making of Empire c. 1820–1840* (Basingstoke: Palgrave, 2011).

Youlden, Harry, 'Shipwreck in Australia', *The Knickerbocker*, Vol. XLI, No. 4 (April 1853), pp. 291–300.

Index